Bedlah, Baubles, and Beads

by
Dawn Devine ~ Davina
and
Barry Brown

IBEXA PRESS

Bedlah, Baubles, and Beads
Copyright © 2001, 2011 Dawn Devine
Book layout and design, Barry Brown
2011 resize and layout, Jerry Case
2011 Cover design, Kristina Reinholds
Front cover artwork, Conrad Wong © 2001
All other illustrations by Dawn Devine © 2001

Published by Ibexa Press
www.ibexa.com

All rights reserved. Reproductions of selected portions of this book is granted for instructional purposes only. Other reproduction in any form by any means must be by consent of the author or publisher.

For more information about books by Dawn Devine aka Davina, please visit her website.
www.davina.us

ISBN-13: 978-0615507040 (Ibexa Press)

Preface

Welcome to *Bedlah, Baubles, and Beads*. This is my third book on designing and making costumes for Middle Eastern Dance. Although popularly recognized by the general public as belly dancing, this dance form has numerous names including *dance oriental* and *raks sharki*. Under these broad categories there are numerous sub-styles that are defined not only by their movement vocabulary, but also by their distinctive costuming.

For most folks, the phrase "belly dancer" conjures up images of dancers in bras and belts with fluffy, full, chiffon skirts. While the details may vary, such as coins vs. beads or fringe vs. swags, the overall perception of the standard costume of the dancer has changed little since the 1950s. But regardless of the popular image of the dancer, only your imagination, sewing skills, time, and budget limit your costume options. No matter if you are a size 2 or 22, there is a costume style to flatter both your figure and your dance style.

While my first book introduced the whole range of belly dance costume, this book focuses almost exclusively on *bedlah*, the highly beaded and embellished bra and belt sets. This style is commonly called *cabaret*, although some dancers use terms like "nightclub," "evening wear," "Las Vegas," or "showgirl." To avoid the negative political and social ramifications of using such a highly charged term as cabaret to describe this beautiful style of dress, I will refer to this style of costuming using an Arabic term, bedlah, which simply means suit. This is the professional uniform of the Middle Eastern dancer and this word seems to be the most appropriate term.

This volume is broken into three parts. Part I provides a conceptual framework for the book by introducing the major themes in dance costume over the last century and then identifies the stylistic features of current design. From there, I go into the mechanics of design, introducing the process, terminology, and techniques of professional designers.

Part II contains chapters on bra and belt construction. Additionally, the mechanics of working with beads, sequins, and rhinestones will be introduced with step-by-step diagrams to help you through the processes of applying these surface design elements.

In Part III, the construction of the foundation garments will be explored. In addition, I have added a few extra chapters to introduce the supporting garments and accessories. To round out this book, I have included a resources list and a selected bibliography.

I hope you find this book informative and entertaining. I wish you luck in all of your costuming adventures.

Happy Costuming!

Dawn Devine ~ Davina

Acknowledgments

I dedicate this book to Barry Brown, co-author, and publisher who has stood by me through the long nights to get this work done. I could never have done it without his skills and his support.

No woman is an island and no book can be produced without the help, guidance, and support of my family, friends, and the dance community. I would like to thank all of the members of Middle Eastern Dance mailing list, the folks over at Gilded Serpent online newsletter, the ladies at Bhuz.com, and all of the print publishers who have accepted and published my writing.

I would like to thank the bevy of friends who have listened to me ponder the big issues and complain about the little ones. Folks like Gretchen Helms, Peggy Beanston, Ian McCloghrie, Nancy Klauschie, Pat Thomas, Matthew and Ami Legare, Niall, and the ladies of Asha of Reno, especially Mary, Chris, and Kay have been invaluable to me. Thanks also go out to The Two Old Bags of Reno, Janie and Chris, who always have a kind word and a dance slot for me. I would like to thank all of the various roomies who have been in and out of my households: Rick, John, Ken, and Scott. And Jerry, you are still distracting me too much with all that bowling, but thanks for being there when I needed you the most.

The members of my on-line artistic support group need to be mentioned! Thank you! Thank you: Lagkitten, Tygger, Tanan, Alendria, Serval, Roon, Hedgy, Susandeer, Pygarr, Doodles, and a host of others too numerous to name. All the years in college haven't taught me nearly as much as the various suggestions and critiques of my fellow artists.

Last but not least, I would like to thank my family who have stood by me and helped to make my dreams come true, especially my Mom who helped edit and stood behind me with motivational words when the writing became tough.

Dawn Davina ~ Davina

About the Contributors

Dawn Devine ~ Davina, author, illustrator

Dawn is a seamstress, costume historian, belly dancer, and author. She currently splits her time between Sacramento and California's Bay Area. She has been belly dancing since 1985. She has degrees in Art History and Costume Design. In her free time, she collects books on costume design, writes articles for dance publications, and makes costumes. Her first book, *Costuming From the Hip,* took the belly dance community by storm in 1997 and is being carried by vendors all over the world. In 2000, she released her second book, *From Turban to Toe Ring,* and has since gone on to start a booklet series and her own web site, www.davina.us.

Barry Brown, editor, layout & design

Computer programmer by day, desktop publisher by night, Barry has been working with computers since 1976. Today, he teaches at a local community college near Sacramento, California. His hobbies include photography (of belly dancers, among other subjects), gardening, cooking, and bicycling.

Conrad Wong, illustrator

Born in Mountain View, California, Conrad graduated from U. C. Berkeley in 1991 and has been following a successful career in the computer industry ever since. He intended to be a best-selling book author but his spare-time interests took a detour through art courtesy of *anime* and with the help of a lot of friends, has been developing his illustrative abilities for fun and a little profit. His remaining spare time is spent going "meow" at random intervals.

Michael Hyde, editor

Michael is a professional editor, technical writer, and historical re-enactor. He lives in the hills above Santa Cruz, California, with his lovely wife, Tish.

For more information about the author and contributors, visit my website at www.davina.us.

Table of Contents

Part I — Design

Introduction 1

1. **History of Dance Costume in the United States** 3
   1890s to Today

2. **Contemporary Styles in Costume** 9
   Tribal • Folkloric • Egyptian • Turkish • Specialty • Gypsy/Fusion

3. **Principles of Design** 15
   Color Theory • Line • Shape • Texture • Patterns • Symmetry • Rhythm
   Unity • Proportion

4. **Designer's Toolbox** 25
   Making a Croquis • Sources of Inspiration • Creating a Portfolio

5. **An Analytic Approach to Designing Bedlah** 31
   Setting Goals • Choosing a Design Motif • Fringe Placement

6. **Designing for Every Body** 37
   Body Analysis • Dominant Figure Types • Emphasizing &
   De-emphasizing Features

Part II — Bedlah Construction and Embellishment

Introduction 45

7. **Bra Construction** 47
   Buying a Bra • Deconstruction • Stabilizing • Covering the Cups
   Decorating

8. **Belt Construction** 57
   Making the Pattern • The Belt Base • Covering the Belt

9. **Surface Embellishments** 63
   Beads • Sequins • Paillettes • Pearls • Coins • Mirrors • Fringe • Supplies

10. **Beading Techniques** 73
    Tambour Beading • Couching • Lazy Stitch • Chain Stitch • Sequins
    Hand Beading

11. **Developing Beaded Designs** 79
    Using Clip Art as a Source • Combining Designs for Variety

Part III — Completing the Look

    Introduction 85

12. **Skirts and Pants** 87
    Harem Pants • Turkish Pants • Salwar • Godets • Straight Skirts
    Tiered Skirts

13. **Accent Garments** 95
    Choli • Vests • Blouses • Hip Wraps • Overskirts

14. **Dresses and Gowns** 101
    Stretch Sheath • Fitted Sheath • Shimmy Dress • Tunic
    Transforming a Store-Bought Dress

15. **Accessories and Embellishments** 107
    Hats • Jewelry • Shoes • Arm Wear • Veils • Wraps • Stomach Covers

16. **Care and Storage** 117

Appendices

    Beadwork Template 120

    Bibliography 121

Part I
Design

Bedlah, the Arabic word for suit, is the most appropriate title for what is, fundamentally, the uniform of the Middle Eastern dancer. The format of the bedlah set, with the elaborately beaded bra and belt supported by a skirt, accent garments, and accessories, was established nearly a century ago. For the past seventy-five years, dancers have experimented, refined, and played with the key features of this style. Changes in coverage, shaping, colors, and design motifs are a natural expression of stylistic evolution. Today, dancers are designing and making their costumes based on tested formulas.

Part I of this book is about the principles and processes that guide the design of bra and belt sets. Being a designer is about making choices. In this section, I introduce an approach to design based on the professional practices of designers in the worlds of theatre and high fashion. From the vocabulary of the designer, sources of inspiration, figure analysis, and problem solving techniques, Part I explores the range of skills a designer needs to create beautifully designed costumes.

Chapter 1 presents a brief overview of the last hundred years of the history and development of bedlah in the United States. The current hottest trends in the world of contemporary costume design are shown in Chapter 2. Chapters 3, 4, and 5 provide the novice designer with the principles and theoretical tools for approaching design projects. Chapter 6 is filled with hints, tips, and ideas for developing designs to flatter a variety of figures.

The goal of Part I is to provide a solid introduction to the tools and techniques of the professional designer. In each section, examples illustrate how these principles can be applied to the design of bedlah. As you read these chapters, try to visualize the process of taking a concept to finished costume. Remember that sewing is just the final step in the design of a garment. The work of the designer begins with that initial spark of inspiration.

History of Dance Costume in the United States

Dance is, by its very nature, an ephemeral art form that exists within a specific moment. Only in the recent past has technology made it possible to record the dance. While, historically, artists have been drawn to the trope of the dancer as a favorite topic for paintings, it was only with the advent of photography and, more specifically, movies and video, that the recording of visual information moved beyond the boundary of the artist's studio. The lens of the camera has documented our dance form throughout the twentieth century.

Early photographs are not an unmediated recording of history. Rather, most photographers used models, not dancers, as their subjects. During the last half of the nineteenth century and first quarter of the twentieth, most images of Middle Eastern women served as pin-ups for a prurient western male gaze. One look at these photographs clearly shows the artificial nature of these images. The backgrounds are almost always staged sets; the poses artfully arranged allusions to motion rather than a slice of an actual dance.

For the costume historian these images are still valuable as a historic document. Most costumes should be viewed as pastiches created from potentially unrelated garments, rather than a direct representation of what one woman wore. Due to the age of the photo, each garment and decoration represents a moment in history. Although it's a highly contrived and suspect whole, the individual parts are worthy of scrutiny. One cannot assume, however, that the costume depicted is an actual dance costume or that the model is a dancer.

From the 1920s through the 1950s and beyond, many burlesque performers adopted costume ensembles from the Middle Eastern design vocabulary to spice up their acts. A researcher must remain keenly aware that not every dancer in belly dance attire from the twentieth century was an actual Middle Eastern dancer. However the costume historian can look at these images and know that what makes them work is the cultural allusion. Belly dance attire by the end of the 1920s had already established a consistent set of features. The bra and belt, skirt, harem pants, beads, jewels, and fringe were, by the forties, part of the formula for the belly dance costume. The burlesque dancer couldn't make a cultural reference work unless the ensemble was already a formulaic and well-established cultural icon.

Where Did Bedlah Originate?

This question comes up again and again, and is a point of debate within the world of Middle Eastern dance. Perhaps we will never know the first dancer or costume designer to adapt a bra for costume purposes and utilize it in a belly dance ensemble. While the origins of Middle Eastern costume are rooted in the Middle East, twentieth century developments are tied to the evolution of showgirl costumes and Hollywood imagery here in the United States. After years of research, I have developed a chronology of the development of dance costumes that traces the arc and development of various design trends and styles. This research has taken me on an exploration of the design influences as they appear in a wide variety of media such as photographs, art works, movies, and videos.

Fashion in dance costume, like all fashion styles, has a myriad of influences that shape each new stylistic innovation. Dancers of all eras, as they do now, take motifs, style lines, and compositions from the world around them, feeling the Zeitgeist, or worldview, and distilling it out through their costumes. The world of costume design is also heavily indebted to the world of technology. As new methods of making beads, rhinestones, and textiles evolved, dancers were quick to embrace the new.

While this one chapter could easily fill an entire book, this summary should give you a good overview of the styles typical of each era. If you find this topic stimulating, and would like to do some research of your own, consult the bibliography for books that can start you off on your own studies.

Last Quarter of the Nineteenth Century

Perhaps the watershed moment for the world of Middle Eastern dance in the United States was the Colombian Exhibition in Chicago in 1893. Although it has been argued that the dancers had already performed in the United States with travelling vaudeville shows, it was this World Fair that brought both the exotic and sublime to the heart of America. There was something for everyone, from the giant Ferris Wheel to the carnival barkers hawking wares and exotic performances. There were exhibits and displays of everything from technological advancements to reform dress. But one of the most infamous of all of the sights was the dance of Little Egypt on the midway. Greeted with negative publicity, the "hootchy-cootchy" dancers of the Chicago midway caused such a stir that cootch dancers began appearing from coast to coast in burlesque shows, carnival side-shows, and dime theatres.

Costume Styles

During the last quarter of the 19th century, dancers performed in costumes composed of a skirt, embellished vest, body stocking, a belt with hanging tabs, jewelry pieces, and a profusion of scarves. Heavy black shoes, small slippers, or boots were worn and the ankles were, rather scandalously, exposed. Complex layers of ethnic jewelry added sparkle and shine to these ensembles. But the feature of the cootch dance costume that made it of extreme prurient interest for the American male was the absence of that most ubiquitous feminine article: the corset.

Costume ca. 1893, Chicago World's Fair.

Milestones in Costuming

Costumes arrived with the dancers themselves. Without dancers there would be no dance costumes! Many of the oldest images of dancers show them standing in line posing. Some dance groups, or individual dancers, will appear to be wearing belts with tabs or ribbons hanging from the waist. This is a visual key that these are images of Gawazee dancers from Egypt. These tabs are one of their signature styles and it's a design feature that will continue to reappear throughout the 20th century.

First Quarter of the Twentieth Century

In the world of modern dance, the Middle East was a trove of concepts and movement vocabulary of great interest to dancers who were trying to break out of the Western ideals of established ballet. Isadora Duncan and Ruth St. Denis brought ethnic inspired dances to the world of "high arts." The Ballet Rousse, with the designs by Leon Bakst, took Arabian exotica into a whole new direction, making it modern and exciting. The Orientalist art movement was experiencing a major revival and Middle Eastern costume seemed fresh to fashion designers such as Erte, Poiret, and Vionnet. At the same time, silent films were making the scene and Valentino was a box office smash, opposite an endless stream of silent harem babes. With the discovery of Tutankhamun's tomb in 1922, a fad for all things Middle Eastern heightened to a frenzy. Egyptomania spread through the major cities of Europe and America like wildfire. Women everywhere wanted clothes that reflected this exotic trend.

Costume worn by Ruth St. Denis, ca. 1910. The chemise had been abandoned by most dancers in the first quarter of the twentieth century.

Assuit is a fabric made of mesh with strips of silver bent, twisted, and hammered down into the structure of the cloth. These silver designs form geometric patterns in the cloth.

Costume Styles

Styles in costume were in transition from the traditional styles, blending, merging, and fusing with both Hollywood Orientalist themes and the glitz and glamour of show-girl costumes. Beads, sequins and rhinestones began appearing during this era, along with the dripping pearls that crossed over from the world of high fashion. Complex and ornately beaded garments became more popular with dancers, and photographs showed a steady progression towards the development of a set formula for Middle Eastern dance costuming. Assuit fabric became a rage in the 1920s and appeared in dance dresses as well as haute couture.

Milestones in Costume

Perhaps the most significant development in the world of the Middle Eastern dance costume occurred in 1921, when a patent for the first bra was issued to a New York socialite who crafted the first bra from a pair of men's hankies and ribbon. Lingerie companies were quick to market this new garment and bras quickly became an important part of ladies clothing. Practically as soon as the structure of the supportive bra was invented, they begin appearing in showgirl and Middle Eastern dance costuming. Be aware that some early costumes depict elaborately decorated metal "bras" are showing garments that rest on the body, not supporting it. Most of these designs were either beaded onto the surface of a dress, vest, or body stocking or they were conceived as elaborate jewelry that covered the chest.

The Thirties, Forties, and Fifties

During this era, most Americans saw images of Middle Eastern dance as background stage filler for movies set in exotic locales. Most of these performances were Hollywood fantasies with costumes crafted in the costume department and dancers pulled from the chorus pool. Alternately, burlesque shows catered to patrons with exotic tastes and used the trope of the exotic Middle Eastern dancer to spice up their performances. During this time, the film industry in Egypt grew in importance, and imported films were arriving in ethnic neighborhoods across the country. Restaurants that featured ethnic foods, from Greek to Moroccan, Turkish to Persian, began sprouting up in more and more large cities. Dancers were hired to draw in crowds eager to soak up the culture. These dancers struggled to preserve the traditional moves while wearing eloquent beaded costumes.

Costume Styles

Styles were less experimental during this era and the bedlah and skirt formula was pretty much set by the 1950s. The dominant styles for surface embellishment included the use of fabric roushing, or pleats, accented with rhinestones and beaded fringe. Skirts were full and fluffy, sheer and chiffon. Bras almost completely replaced the beaded and embellished vest as the principle top garment. Photographs of costumes from this era clearly showed that costume bras followed the same style lines fashionable for lingerie bras. The bustline was lifted and separated, with little cleavage and, by today's standards, a rather high cut through the tops of the cups.

Milestones in costume

The influence of the showgirl style of costume became much more evident during this time. The use of elaborate beading and beaded fringe on the bra and belt became an established formula along with the development of the "classic" three-circle skirt. The showgirl look with immaculate makeup, elegant high-heels, rhinestones, and beads was the look of the day. In many costumes from this era the only apparent difference between a showgirl costume and a Middle Eastern dance costume was the presence of a full-length skirt.

The Sixties and Seventies

During the 1960s the fad for belly dance exploded. While professional dancers were performing at one of the many ethnic restaurants in major cities, classes were popping up at the local YWCA. Middle Eastern dance became popular with young women exploring alternative modes for expressing their femininity. Belly dance became a popular recreational dance form for women seeking to add grace and sensuality to their lives. Movies continued to spotlight dancers as set dressing in the backgrounds of exotic locales, but unlike the 1940s and 1950s, the quality of these dancers improved. This was also the era of *I Dream of Jeannie* and the harem fantasy continued as a sub theme among women learning to dance. Through the 1970s the number of musical works available on album expanded and books on belly dance for home study hit the market. By the middle of the 1970s the seeds of the belly dance culture,

1950s-era Egyptian style costume. By midcentury, the bra had almost totally replaced the fitted vest.

By the late 1960s, skirts became more abbreviated and the belt rode low on the hips.

Fantasy gypsy with coin bra and belt and circle skirt with flounce.

as a distinct group, began to form with dance festivals, publications, and social groups forming across the country, but especially in New York, San Francisco, and Los Angeles.

Costume Styles

During this era two major styles were popular. On the one hand, there was a "fantasy Gypsy" style that that featured an abundant use of rayon fringe and coins. Full fluffy skirts, lace shawls, hip wraps, or coin belts worn with strappy halter-style bras or loose blouses typified this style. There was an abundance of layered fabric, sometimes in bright prints, but with lots of color and movement. Alternately, beads and sequined costumes continued to be the popular choice for professional dancers.

Milestones in Costume

Venues for historical recreation began appearing across the United States. Renaissance festivals and the development of the Society for Creative Anachronism (SCA) created new opportunities for dancers to perform. The tribal style, a fusion of history and contemporary styles from rural, nomadic, and traditional cultures developed in response to these new performance opportunities. Fantasy Gypsy styles reached a peak of popularity as the fresh new dance look, giving performers an alternative to the glamorous, but expensive, beaded and sequined costumes.

The Eighties and Nineties

By the early 1980s, popular interest in Middle Eastern dance had blossomed into an active and vibrant dance community. Belly dance magazines with national and international circulation linked these communities and brought news of the hottest trends, performance venues, and festivals throughout the United States. In major cities, organizations formed to provide the interested hobbyist with information, instructors, events, and vendors. As a backlash to stressful and non-creative aerobic style dance, women turned to belly dance as a low-strain method for keeping fit, exploring their creative side, and connecting with a larger community of women. With the growth of the videotape industry and a drop in the cost of video production, dancers begin putting together instructional videos. These tapes expanded the dancer's fame out from their locale and superstars begin to develop within the dance community. By the 1990s it became relatively easy for students to take workshops hosted by local instructors with stars from across the U.S. and overseas.

With tightening restrictions on dance costume in Egypt and influence of designers such as Bob Mackie and Halston, the 1980s saw a surge in elaborately beaded dance dresses.

Costume Styles

Imported costumes became easier to acquire during the 1980s and 1990s. The ateliers of Egypt and Turkey dominated the world of dance by making extravagant beaded bedlah and dresses. These glamorous costumes were big-ticket items and a brisk second hand market sprouted up as teachers sold their gently-used costumes to students. More and more dancers began to experiment with new styles and the traditional styles, cabaret, folkloric, and tribal are defused and expanded upon. The evening soap operas of the early 1980s such as *Dynasty* and *Dallas* fueled a fever for rhinestones and expensive full-length gowns. Almost as a backlash, a keep-it-simple style that was built from practice wear became established. Easy-to-wear tiered skirts, body suits, or choli with a simple beaded hip sash were popular for both practice and performance. And finally, the development of the Internet has allowed dancers all over the world to contact each other, exchange stylistic information, and see what the latest trends are with a simple push of a button.

Milestones in Costume

The development of Spandex changed the quality of fit in formal gowns and dance dresses. Straight skirts that clung to the thigh and yet still allowed for a wide range of motions radically changed the silhouette of the performance costume. Also, new technologies have allowed for the development of adhesive products that can extend the life of costumes. Holographic foil changed the world of sequins and paillettes by proving to be sweat resistant, making them not only more sparkly, but longer lasting as well. The popularity of beaded jewelry sparks the expansion of bead stores throughout the country, allowing dancers to find materials for making glitzy costumes in their own communities. Through mail order and vendors on the Internet, anyone can order the materials needed to create beautiful and complex ensembles.

This is a typical ensemble suitable for practice wear. It includes a stretch choli, hip wrap, and harem pants. This has become the "uniform" of the student dancer in the 90s.

2 Contemporary Styles

Only your imagination and budget limit the options available in contemporary Middle Eastern dancewear. There is literally something for everyone! However, with such expansive options, it can be difficult to narrow down a selection, much less to define what you are looking at. This chapter serves as a summary of the most popular styles worn by dancers today. While this list cannot possibly cover every subtle permutation in the world of Middle Eastern costume design, it does introduce the major themes.

Egyptian

Egyptian costumes fall into two camps. There are the bedlah-based costumes, which often feature quite flamboyant decorative programs with large appliques and beaded designs. The bras and belts tend to have simplistic shapes, although more complex pieces are available. There is an extensive use of thickly beaded fringe, which often falls in waves from the bra and belt. The surfaces of the cloth are elaborately beaded with bugle beads, sequins, and rhinestones.

Beledi dresses are another major stylistic group available from Egyptian designers. Beledi dresses range from the informal to the glamorous, folkloric to high fashion. They often feature sexy cutouts, appliqués, complex beading and embroideries with exciting hem treatments. These dresses are available in stretch fabrics, or have complex princess seams to provide fit and shaping. Overall, Egyptian styles are elegant and refined but often feature large design motifs, bright color combinations, and narrow skirts with deep ruffles from the knees down.

Turkish

Turkish style costumes utilize the bedlah format as a principal design element. Turkish styles tend to extend beyond the edges of the costume using appliques and wire to build up different shapes along the cups of the bra or the edges of the belt. Some costume designers tend to make more revealing pieces such as straight slit skirts, narrow bra straps and few accessory garments. To meet the needs of different tastes, Turkish designers make beladi dresses as well, focussing on the use of stretch garments with lots of revealing cutouts. In general, Turkish styles are sexy, spicy, and more revealing than their Egyptian counterparts.

American

Dancers in the United States are masters of ingenuity and frequently pick and choose design elements, costume pieces, and accessories from a variety of different sources to create individualistic styles. Many dancers purchase a bedlah set and then make the accessory pieces to coordinate and expand their wardrobe. American costumes will frequently include coordinated veils that match or harmonize with skirts and pants. Dancers who build their own costumes will design ensembles that are best for their own figures and styles of dance. There are many designers in the United States who create costumes with a purely American aesthetic, with an emphasis on the traditional classic three-circle panel skirt and long flowing rectangular or circular veils.

Contemporary Styles

Gypsy/Fusion

This style is a fantasy melange of standard dance wear forms with colors, skirt cuts, and design elements worn by the Romany peoples of the Mediterranean region. From Andalusia to Turkey, the features of Gypsy/Fusion styles are based on easily recognizable sets of design features. The bra and belt relies on braid, coins, and fringe for the decoration rather than beads and sequins. Other elements include fitted under-the-bust vests, blouses with full, ruffled sleeves, and contrasting hip wraps with fringe worn below the belt. Colors are frequently dark, using a good deal of black as a base, with jewel tones and lots of pattern and texture.

Flamenco Influences

Similar in style to Gypsy/Fusion, Flamenco style costumes incorporate many of the design features favored by Flamenco dancers. They range from the big chunky shoes to the use of polka dots and cabbage roses, in black, red, white, and yellow. Skirts are cut narrow through to the thighs but then begin to widen below the knees using gores or godets. Full dresses, blouses that tie below the bust, and sleek smooth hair are features easily identifiable as Flamenco inspired. Lace is a hallmark textile, especially in black. Shawls made of lace and skirts with tiers of lace ruffles and layered effects with rich colors showing through are part of the look.

Tribal Style

The tribal style of costuming uses a different format for its costumes than the standard bedlah bra and belt. Tribal dancers do wear bras, but instead of covering them with beads or coins, they utilize tribal jewelry pieces, charms, tokens, and other metal parts to create a look that is totally unique. The tribal bra is generally worn layered over a choli or under a vest. Rather than a fitted belt, tribal dancers frequently utilize a front or side tying layered hip wrap ensemble. The top layer is frequently used as a field for the display of imported textiles, jewelry parts, shi-sha work and tassels. The look is at once eclectic, wildly layered, and visually complex.

Indian Essences

Many dancers have access to lovely sari fabrics for creating dancewear. While sari cloth can be used in virtually any style of costuming, from glitzy cabaret to earthy tribal, the flavors of India can be integrated into the cut and styling of the garments. What design features create this look? It's the fitted choli styles that match or coordinate with the skirt. A coordinated look, with all of the costume pieces cut from the same cloth, or from coordinating pieces, helps to underscore the Indian style. Pants, cut in a draped shalwar style, can be a focal point with a half skirt behind to frame the legs. A straight skirt with the sari border used as a linear element down the seams, the slits, or at the hem can be an alternative to full pleated or gathered skirts.

Contemporary Styles

Vintage Looks

Vintage costumes are based on styles from the last one hundred years. Vintage looks cover a broad range, from re-creations of costumes worn by infamous dancers such as "Little Egypt" and "Mata Hari" to updated styles based on the costumes of Egyptian dancers of the 1940s and 1950s. Just as the world of high fashion pillages the past for retro looks, so too can the dance costumer look back across time for inspiration. Designers can be inspired by the numerous early movies of the 1910s and 1920s which capitalized on the American taste for Orientalist themes and featured exotic costumes that can provide a wealth of inspiration.

Historical Styles

There are many dancers who perform at historical reenactments. SCA events, Renaissance and medieval faires provide venue for dancers. Depending on the era being depicted and the culture selected, these costumes can vary wildly in look and feel. Since bedlah is based on the modern costume device, the bra, it's not historically accurate for pre-twentieth century costuming. However, many dancers blend history with contemporary garments, and seasoned with a liberal dosage of design elements pulled from Orientalist paintings of the 18th and 19th centuries. Generally, this style features the use of a center-opening robe, called an anteri, but when cut below the bust it is more familiarly known as a gawazee coat. Khaftans and other closed dresses cut from traditional materials are also frequently spotted at these events, as are folkloric and tribal styles.

Specialty Costumes

Specialty costumes can be fun to perform in and help to tie into the theme of a special event. A standard bedlah and skirt combination can frequently be transformed into a specialty look with the use of headwear, arm treatments, and jewelry. Some common specialty styles include pharaonic, goddess themes, and elemental themes such as water, fire, and air. Events and seasons can present opportunities for themed costumes. Think of how you can transform a single costume. For example, a single red costume can suit a wide variety of holidays. On Valentine's Day, it can be worn with a pink skirt and heart-motif accessories. On the Fourth of July, Flag Day, or other national holiday it can be coordinated with a blue and white skirt and vest in stripes or solid colors. And then around Christmas time, this same bedlah set, worn with green accessories and accented with sparkling gold ribbons and trim, is the perfect ensemble.

Folkloric

Folkloric styles of dance costumes cross the boundaries of both tribal and historical. Folkloric costumes are based on the traditional clothing styles of specific peoples from around the Middle East and are worn when performing culturally significant styles of dance. There is a broad range of Folkloric styles due to the tremendous sweep of cultures that get grouped under the umbrella term "Middle Eastern dance." From the Guedra of Morocco to the Kaleegee dances of the Arabian Gulf there are numerous dances that require a specific style of costume to support the look and style of the dance.

3 Principles of Design

This chapter briefly introduces the basic principles of design. For the trained designer, this will be a review. The average seamstress may intuitively understand the elements and principles of design and how to manipulate them. For others, the following pages might introduce enough new vocabulary to sound like a foreign language! This chapter defines a common vocabulary for design concepts used in the worlds of costume and fashion design. These terms will make holding an informed discussion of costuming possible. This section does, by no means, take the place in a serious course on costume or fashion design. However, this chapter should give you a taste of design principles and a foundation for further exploration. I recommend consulting the sewing section of the bibliography for more resources on costume and fashion design.

Design Concepts

What does it mean to design? At its most basic:

Design is the process of using the principles of design to organize and arrange the elements of design.

Many costume makers intuitively see the pattern and organization of design features within a complete ensemble. All garments are composed of building blocks of textiles, sequins, and beads. But there are two design concepts that form an underlying conceptual framework for discussing the process of creating new styles.

The **elements of design** are the building blocks that are systematically arranged to create new and exciting garments. These elements are **color, line, shape, pattern,** and **texture.**

The **principles of design** are the rules that guide the organization of the design elements. These include **proportion, balance, rhythm, emphasis,** and **unity.**

But, perhaps, the term "rule" is too strict; rather, consider these as guiding principles which will give you a method for thinking about design.

Elements of Design

The elements of design are the building blocks of the design world. These five essential design features appear in every costume. These are all features that we can see and experience visually. When you look at a costume, try to break it into its separate parts.

Examine this bedlah set. Do you think it is an effective costume? Read this chapter and look at this costume again. What design principles and elements do you see at work?

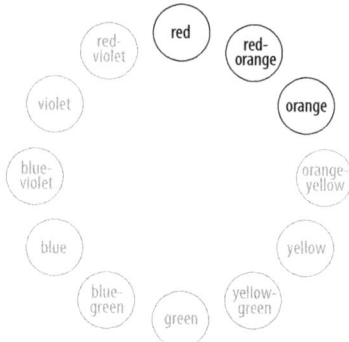

Analogous colors.

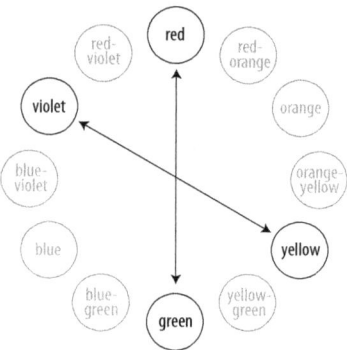

Complimentary colors.

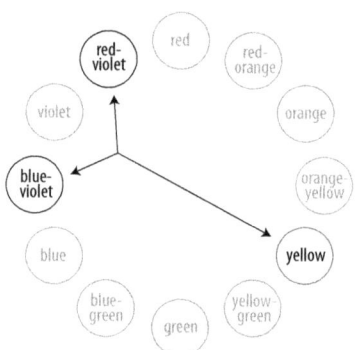

Split complimentaries.

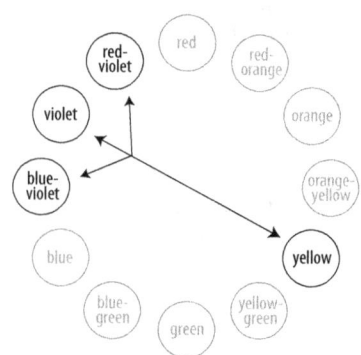

Analogous complimentary colors.

Color

It is very difficult to discuss color in the pages of a black and white book. But color is one of the most important design elements. It transmits mood and feeling and is most easily manipulated using the principles listed below. A color wheel is an excellent tool, available in craft or art stores. A good color wheel will help you to gain a better understanding of how colors work.

Colors are defined in three ways:

Hue. This is the technical name for color. A **tint** is a hue with white added; **tone** is a hue with gray added; and a **shade** is a hue with black added.

Value is the lightness or darkness of a color.

Intensity is the brightness or dullness of a color.

The color wheel is a map of the relationships of the colors. Color theory has been employed by artists, designers, and crafts people in their work since the nineteenth century.

Primary Colors. These are the colors that cannot be formed by mixing other hues. There are three primary colors: **red, blue,** and **yellow.**

Secondary Colors. These are hues that are formed by mixing two primaries together.

Red + Blue = Violet
Blue + Yellow = Green
Red + Yellow = Orange

Tertiary Colors. These are formed by mixing together a secondary color and one of its neighboring primary colors.

Red + Violet = Red-violet
Orange + Red = Red-orange

The colors relate to each other in a variety of different ways. A **color scheme** is formed whenever you place two or more colors in proximity in the same project. Here are some of the technical terms for the most popular color scheme groupings.

Monochromatic. This is a color scheme that uses one color, but with a variety of tints, tones and shades. (Red and pink.)

Analogous. This is a color scheme composed of two or more colors that are directly touching on the color wheel. (Red, red-orange, orange.)

Achromatic. This is a colorless scheme that uses shades of gray. (Black, white, light gray.)

Complimentary. These are schemes that use colors directly opposite each other on the color wheel. (Violet and yellow or red and green.)

Split complementary. Using the colors on either side of the complement. (Yellow with red-violet and blue-violet.)

Analogous complimentary. Using a color, its complement, and the two closest neighbors. (Yellow, violet, red-violet and blue-violet.)

Principles of Design

Diad. Two colors that are two spaces apart on the wheel. (Red, orange.)

Triad. Three colors equally spaced (Red, blue, yellow.)

Tetrad. Four colors evenly distributed around the wheel. (Red, yellow, violet, green.)

In the world of Middle Eastern dance costume, there are some well-established conventions for using color in costume design. One of the most popular formulas for dance costume colors scheming is:

Main color + Accent color + Metallic = Beautiful costume!

Main color. No matter how simplistic or complex, you will have to select a color for your costume. Dancers new to the world of design often select one of the "standard" colors for dance costume. Red, black, deep blue, emerald green, and white seem to have a staying power, enduring the test of time.

Accent Colors. Black and white are frequently used as accent colors because they will automatically coordinate with any color of the rainbow. Many dancers will extend the options of their wardrobes by selecting costumes with only one primary hue and adding one or two of the neutral accents. A red and black costume, for instance, can be easily accented with either black or red accent pieces and accessories.

Metallic. Silver, gold, copper, brass, and other metallic tones are frequently used as an accent in monochromatic schemes. Many dancers rely on the luster of metal to add sparkle and shine to their costumes.

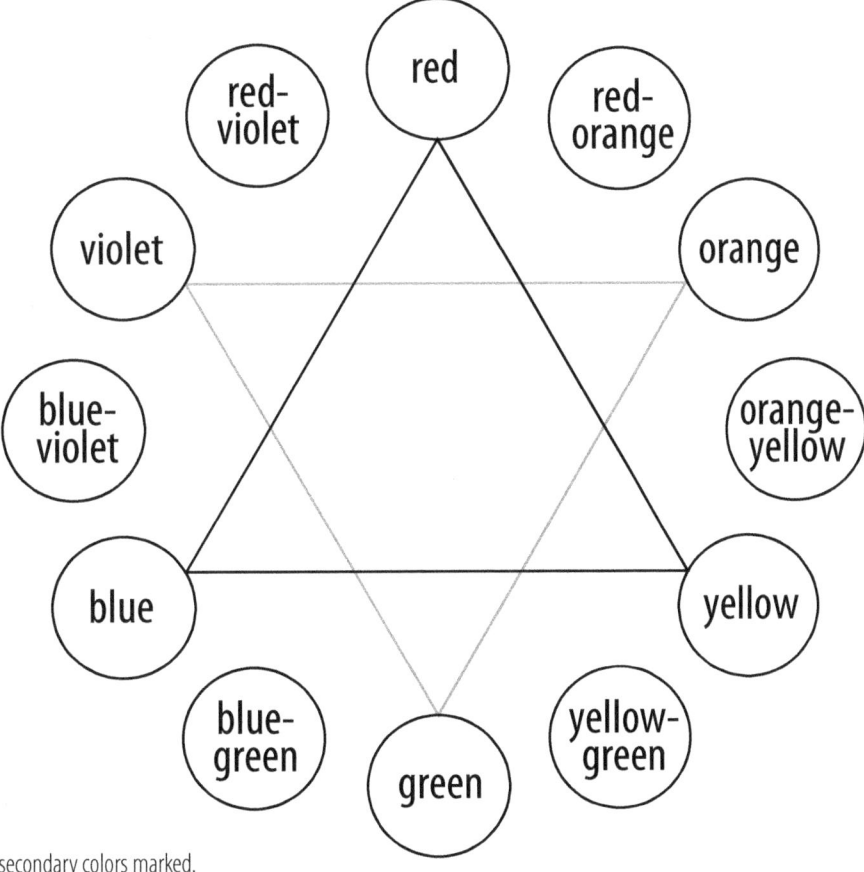

The color wheel, with primary and secondary colors marked.

Line Vocabulary

Straight, curved, angular, zigzag, wavy, swoopy, staccato.

Line

While a dot is the smallest unit of design, the line is the most fundamental element of design. Lines appear where two design elements collide. Lines delineate the structure and contours of shapes. They can create mood through the quality of their contours. From sharp and jagged to smooth and flowing, the line can be manipulated in infinite ways to create the boundaries that define different spaces in a costume. Lines are also a part of the surface design process creating patterns and visual textures in cloth.

Lines are extremely important for the designer because they can be manipulated in such a way as to draw the viewer's eye around the costume. Many optical illusions can be created using the interior lines of the garments, the shape of the edges of the garment, and the surface design patterning.

Vertical lines. These elongate the body because the eye follows the line up and down. Strong vertical lines can instantly make any dancer's figure appear taller and more slender. Curved lines that end pointing upwards or downwards will lead the viewer's eye into a vertical motion.

Horizontal lines. These lines emphasize width. The belt draws a very natural horizontal line across the hips. If this line is shaped, it can minimize the effects of cutting the body in two and making the hips seem even wider. Straight-cut hip belts will visually widen the body. So, too, will horizontal lines across the bra emphasize the size of the bust.

Diagonal lines. The neckline of the dance bra almost always features a diagonal line. These can be dynamic, dramatic, and, if they are more vertical in look, slimming for the dancer's figure. Diagonal lines can be effectively used with vertical lines to effectively move the eye to specific focus areas.

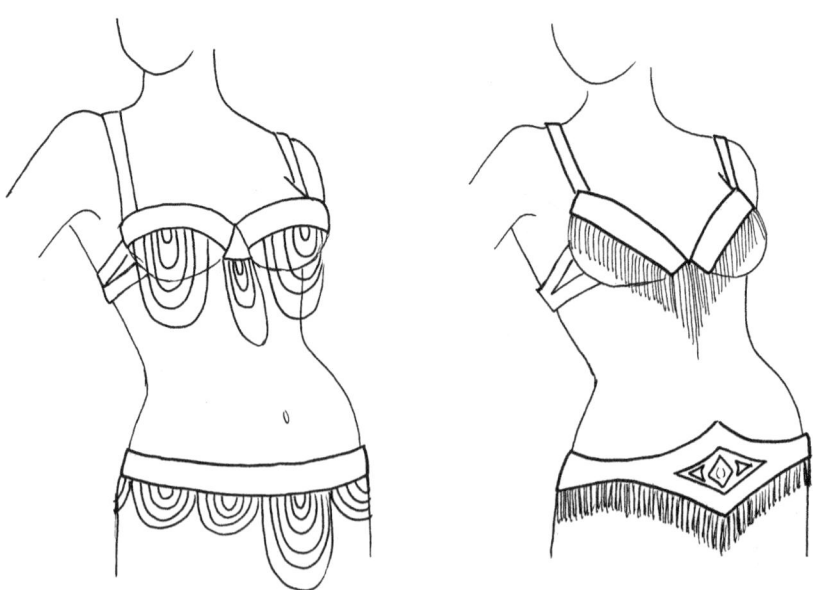

Notice the different lines used. Left: horizontal and swoops. Right: angles and verticals.

Principles of Design

Shape Vocabulary

Angular, circular, diamond, square, oval, scooped.

Shape

Each piece of your costume creates an individual shape. In the world of fashion we refer to the outside shape as the *silhouette*. Internal shapes can be created within these larger expanses. But unlike line, which is closely related, shape indicates a two-dimensional field of color or pattern. Since dance costumes are often created from multiple garments, it's important to carry the same shapes throughout the various pieces. The bra and belt should have similar shaping or they can appear mismatched, even when made from the same materials.

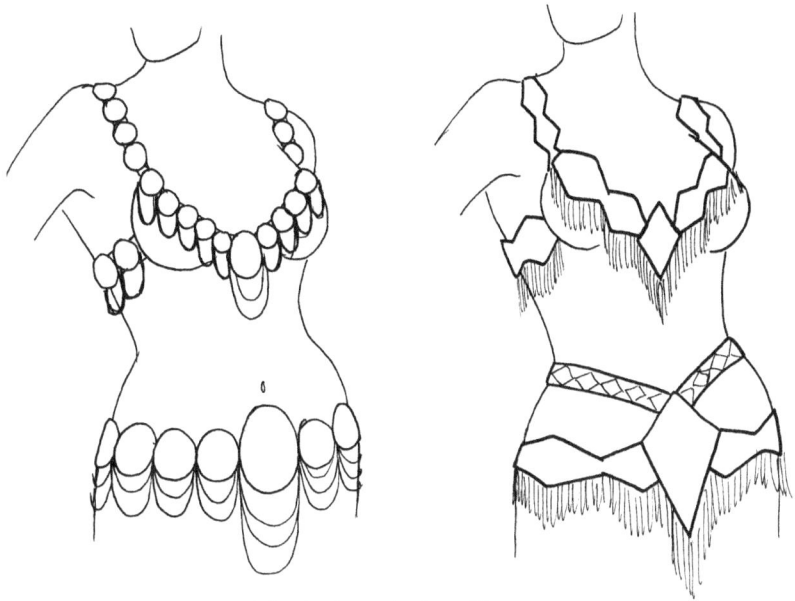

Left: Circular shapes dominate this costume.
Right: Diamond shapes change the visual dynamics of the costume.

Pattern

Pattern can be introduced into the costume in two basic ways: through the use of patterned cloth or applied as a surface design. Patterned fabric can create visual interest within the costume when contrasted with different textures and color. Scale (see below) must always be a consideration when working with patterned fabrics.

Surface design. These are the patterns that you build up on the surface of your garment, such as the beading, braid, and trim added to the bra and belt set. It is important when using pattern on your bra and belt that you echo the patterns between the top and the bottom.

Scale. An important point to remember about patterned fabric is that they come in different sizes. The pattern of the cloth should be scaled to suit your individual body proportions. For instance, a petite dancer can be overwhelmed by a large, all-over print skirt that would look stunning on a larger or more full-figured dancer. Larger sized florals or geometrics will appear to cover larger expanses, giving the impression of a larger figure—not necessarily a goal of most costumers.

Pattern Vocabulary

Stripes, dots, swirls, paisley, plaid, floral, geometric.

Left: Large scale floral print.   Right: Small scale stripe.

Texture Vocabulary

Soft, shiny, silky, smooth, ridged, bumby, slubby, rough, woven, nappy, fluffy, fuzzy.

In these two ensembles, the belts and bras don't match. Think about the relative sizes of the pieces. In the top image, the belt appears too narrow when compared to the bra and will emphasize a large bust. Below, the belt seems too thick and will end up emphasizing the hips.

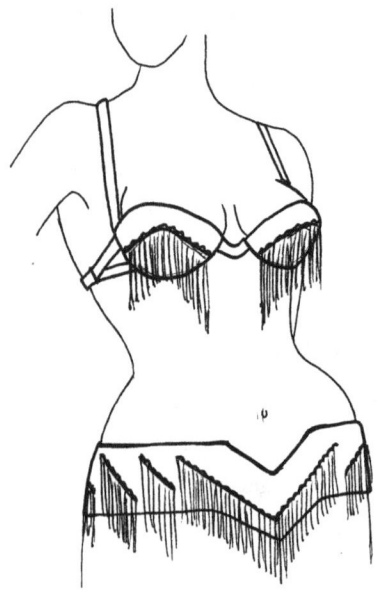

Texture

In costume design, texture can be created in several ways. Applied surface design creates texture with contrasts in beads, sequins, gems and jewels. Texture is also introduced into the costume in the form of patterned decorative fabrics. Texture is about how light reflects off of the garment and the way the eye perceives the subtle differences created by different materials and media. Texture is created by the structure of the cloth, the drape or hand of the fabric, and the surface treatments.

Contrasts in texture, even when the cloth is the same color, will add interest to your garment by giving the viewers a change to perceive. Changes in texture can be highlighted as a feature, using braid or trim to delineate between the areas, or these changes can bump up against each other, creating a line of demarcation.

Principles of Design

Proportion

Proportion, at its most basic, is simply the relationship between one part of the costume to the whole garment. Basic human proportion is based on an average of 8.5 heads tall. This means that head is approximately one eighth of the entire body. When you look at yourself in the mirror, you might see your own personal variations on these ideal proportions. You might feel that your arms are too long, your legs too short, or your feet too big. Costuming gives you the power to shape the way viewers look at your body. Manipulating proportion is one of the best ways to guide the eye around your figure.

When it comes to dance costumes, maintaining good proportions with the body can be very important. A costume with narrow bra straps and a thin belt might give the overall costume a tenuous and unsupported look, revealing more of the body than is necessary. Larger bodies require thicker belts, more fully shaped bras, and more substantial skirts to maintain the proportion of the body. Conversely, petite dancers can be overwhelmed by costumes with thicker belts and long, heavy, beaded fringe designs.

Proportion can be manipulated to draw attention to features you want to play up. A large decorative motif, for instance, placed on the shoulder region will draw the eye up to this region. It is the contrast between the proportions of the other design elements and the focal point which draws the eye.

Emphasis

Emphasis is the act of drawing the eye to a particular location, element, or feature of the design. Emphasis is created through developing contrasts in size, shape, color, and texture. Creating focal points that will pull the eye to specific location allow you, the designer, to control where the viewer will look. This can be done easily by developing a strong design motif. While smaller motifs can be used throughout the costume to coordinate all of the elements, one single large motif can create a show-stopping focal point.

Principles of Design

Rose motif with large central focal point.

Focal point. A focal point can exist in any piece of the costume. It's the design element or garment feature that is the most important, in size, shape, color, or texture. When there is a distinctive focal point, the eye will unconsciously be drawn there and may have difficulty breaking away. As a designer, your job will be to create costumes with interesting focal points that aren't overpowering.

Design motif. The use of a design motif is one of the easiest ways to tie a costume together. The motif is a design element that is repeated throughout the garment. It can be anything from a geometric shape, floral pattern, or a recognizable iconic image, such as a heart, a cat, or a paisley.

Rhythm

Rhythm is the use of design lines to create patterns and textures. Creating repeated design elements that tie a costume together also helps develop rhythm. Repetition of design elements, motifs or textures create a unified look throughout the costume, even though individual costume pieces might be separated by expanses of the body.

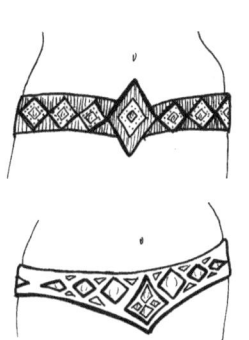

Repetition is the use of the same design elements throughout a design. This is the most easily identified and simple to use design principle, and one that you need to be careful of. It is easy to make a costume appear visually boring through high repetition of small details with no main focal point.

Gradation is the gradual change of one design element into another, which guides the movement of the viewer's eye. Attention will flow across the costume following this change. Any of the elements of design can be used in gradation to segue from one design area to another.

Balance

Balance is often called symmetry, although symmetry is just one version of balance. Balance is about creating a garment where all of the design features and elements coexist without one part becoming too overly dominant. While a focal point is important for creating emphasis, if you go overboard in scale the costume will not be well balanced. The easiest way to maintain good balance is to select and use one form of symmetry throughout the ensemble. **Symmetry** is the organization or division of the design elements into equal parts.

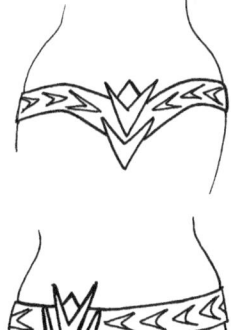

Bilateral symmetry is the most common form of symmetry and the way that the human body is organized. There is a central line that goes down the middle, and on either side of this line the elements are mirrored. Your face is one example of bilateral symmetry, with the nose aligned down the middle, and your eyes and ears mirrored on either side of the face. By their very nature, bras are bilaterally symmetrical garments.

Asymmetry is the use of design elements in an off centered design to effectively create a dynamic tension. The eye will instantly go to the design element that is positioned asymmetrically, especially when the bulk of the decoration is symmetrical. Asymmetrical design elements can be positioned over otherwise symmetrical garment shapes to change the way the eye moves

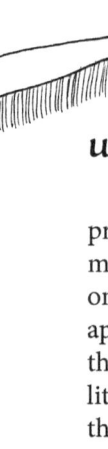

Notice how the diamond motif is repeated throughout the costume pieces, creating visual unity.

around the costume. Select one or two points on the costume where you want to build an asymmetrical design. If you select more than two, the costume can become visually unbalanced.

Unity

Unity is the perfect integration of all of the design elements and design principles to create an effective costume. A costume can have great design motifs, be a fabulous color, and the cut and construction impeccable, but if one of the design elements is overpowering or forgotten, the costume might appear overworked or unfinished. Accessories can have a profound impact on the ultimate look of the costume. When you are designing, consider all of the little details and how they will integrate into the entire ensemble. Consider the jewelry, hair ornamentation, and even the cosmetics that will be worn with the ensemble. Unity is about the total look and requires a designer to think in terms of all of the various parts and pieces throughout the costume. Think three-dimensionally. Avoid designing only "a front and back;" remember that there is a side and that viewers will see you in the round.

The Process of Design

Experienced designers develop a process for taking their ideas and concepts from a simple sketch to a final product. How does one develop a design? Where can a new designer begin? There are as many different "processes" as there are designers. What works for some may not work for you. Developing an individual process will take trial and error, but once you find your method, you will discover that designing beautiful costumes is an easy and repeatable process. To get you started, here is one general scheme that might inspire the development of your own design process.

Inspiration. Something triggers the initial idea or concept for a costume. This idea can be generated by nearly anything from a color scheme to the specific cut or line of a garment or even a design motif or surface embellishment treatment. Other dance costumes, ethnic clothing, and high fashion are all potent tools for triggering ideas for costumes. But don't feel limited to looking only at other garments. How about the flowers in the garden, architecture, or travel photography? Nearly anything can inspire. Let your mind run wild!

Initial sketch. Use your personal croquis or a reference figure (see Chapter 4, the Designer's Toolbox) to record your initial ideas. Even if this is just a concept for a single motif or design element, draw the details. If it's an image from a magazine or book, get a color photocopy and stick it in your sketchbook. This first sketch is to get the most critical or inspirational information onto paper. The shape of the belt and bra, the line of the skirt, and the neckline of a dress are all the kinds of information you want to get into this first sketch.

Initial sketch.

Principles of Design

Refined design.

Rework and develop. Take your initial sketch and start to add details, working and reworking your basic concept. Take your sketches further, drawing back, front, and side views. This might be the time that you play with the size and placement of the motifs. Use colored pencils or markers to get some ideas about color and color placement.

Swatching. The next step is to go shopping for materials. This is the point where you collect samples of surface embellishments and swatches of fabrics needed to create the costume. If you have a wonderful concept but cannot find a particular fabric, appliqué, or trim, you won't be able to make the costume. Swatching trips are your reality check. They also allow you to double check your budget. Can you afford to make the design of your dreams?

Finalize the design. Once you have your materials selected and know what is available, finalize your design sketch. Many designers attach their swatches and samples of their trims, beads, and other materials right onto the sketch. At this stage, you will also make your to-do list for shopping and construction. Your to-do list will establish which pieces you make and in what order you construct them.

Shop. Before you can make your costume, you have to go out and buy all the materials and supplies. Make sure to wear comfortable shoes and stick to your budget. If you overspend you might wind up resenting your costume, so stay within your means when doing your shopping.

Create the garments. This will take the most time and energy. When you are planning your project, consider how long it will take you to manufacture the various parts and pieces. It's impossible to, for example, whip up a beaded gown over a weekend. It's important to set realistic goals for yourself. If you have a deadline, consider making the most important pieces first.

Document the costume. Once you have completed the costume, make sure to arrange to have photos taken of your finished garment. This is especially important to schedule when working with clients. While a professional photo shoot is ideal, just getting some snapshots is important to record what you have done. Try to get photos of the front, back, and sides of the costume both when still and in motion. If you are building a portfolio, have enlargements made.

Process of Design Flowchart

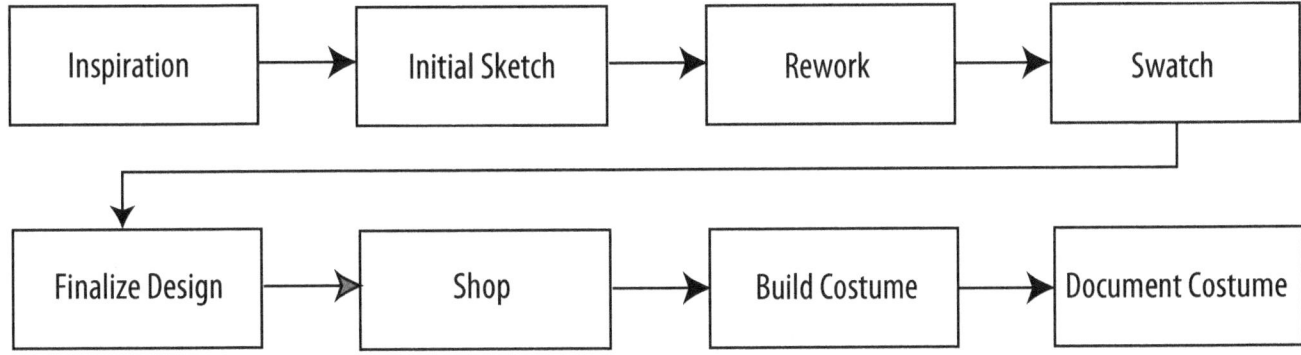

Two examples of stock figures, a drawing tool.

4 Designer's Toolbox

While an understanding of the basic principles of design is key to developing effective costumes, there are many tools and techniques that will make it easier to visualize your designs. In this chapter, I will be introducing several of the most valuable tools and practices that professional designers use to streamline the creative process.

Drawing

There is a myth that designers have an intrinsic talent for drawing. In my years at college, as both a student and instructor, I can say with great certainty that drawing is a skill that can be learned. For a costume designer, the drawings you make don't have to be fine art. A drawing is a tool used to communicate the essential elements of your costume. Drawing gives you a chance to test styles, cuts, and features before spending lots of money in materials and time in construction.

Many professional designers use reference figures, called croquis, or stock figure, to sketch on. These models provide the artist with a well-proportioned body, alleviating the stress of drawing a "person." Keeping a selection of figures in a variety of different poses will allow you to translate ideas from your mind onto paper. A sketch can help you work out some of the finer points of the design. You can test the placement and look of design features. How long will the stomach drape be? Where will fringe be placed? How big should an appliqué be? Even if your drawings are just a set of basic lines with some circles, squares, and triangles, you can add notes to help you get all of your ideas down.

Drawing doesn't need to be an expensive process. A standard #2 pencil and a sketchbook will get you started. Look for images to turn into stock figures with interesting poses, views, and shapes. Scour fashion magazines and use artist's tracing paper to go over the lines of the figures. Take the time to sketch a little each week and you will develop both your drawing and design skills. Keeping your drawings together in a sketchbook or binder will help you track your progress and allow you to see your designs develop and evolve. There are many books available that can help you get started with the basic principles of drawing. Several of my favorite titles are listed in the art section of the bibliography.

Transferring the Croquis to Your Sketch Paper

There are two main methods for transferring images onto other paper: with light or with a transfer medium. Professional designers use a light table to transfer their croquis to their drawing paper. Laying the darkly-lined figure on the table, they place their drawing paper over it. The light shows the

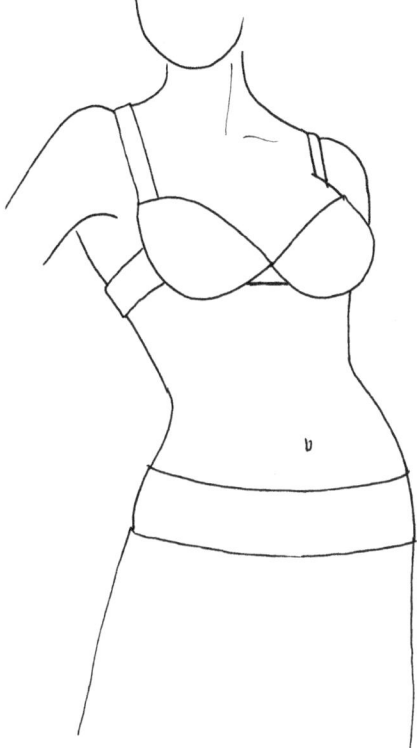

I have used this stock figure throughout the book. The 3/4 twist allows the bra to be seen from the front and side.

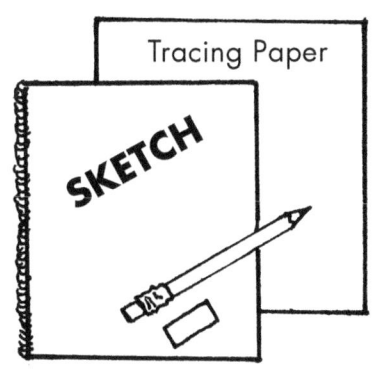

lines from the image below, allowing the designer to trace the figure. Since most folks don't have a light box lying around, you might need to improvise. Putting a light under a glass table is one method. If you have a window, you can place your croquis and the paper against the pane and let natural sunlight shine through, illuminating the figure beneath.

An alternate method is to use a transfer medium. Going over the backside of the paper that has the croquis on it with a very soft pencil prepares it to make a transfer. You then turn the image over and trace over the lines of the drawing. This presses the pencil from the back onto your drawing paper below. Another option is to use carbon paper or even fabric tracing paper. Simply sandwich the transfer medium between the croquis and the drawing paper and draw over the lines of the figure.

Another transfer method is simply to photocopy your croquis and draw your designs directly on the copy. You can use a three-hole punch to store your sketches in a three-ring binder, or you can slide them into the three-hole plastic sleeves used to store comic books. If you have an established sketchbook, you can still draw on photocopies—simply tape them into place in the sketchbook. When you draw directly on a photocopy, you might find there are lines you want to eliminate, such as the legs. Use a whiteout pen to eliminate the features, re-photocopy your drawing, and poof! they are gone.

Don't be afraid to draw your ideas. Even simple drawings can give you good ideas.

Developing a Personalized Croquis

Drawing your sketches on a figure that closely matches your own proportions and shape can make visualizing your costumes easier. Developing a personalized croquis might be the best option if you have figure challenges and your proportions differ dramatically from stock figures. If you have developed your drawing skills, you may want to just whip up a drawing of yourself using a photograph of yourself as a reference. If you are more tentative about your drawing skills, you can create a croquis of your body by directly tracing a photograph.

To Create a Croquis

Step 1: Have photographs taken of yourself. Wear close-fitting garments such as a body suit, unitard, a tight shirt, and leggings. The photographs should be full length, with the body occupying the largest possible portion of the photograph frame. Take two front views: one with your feet shoulder width apart and your weight balanced, a second with your weight shifted to one side and perhaps with a leg extended. In the second image have your arms artfully positioned, with one extended. Continue with side and back shots. Remember to include a balanced and weight-shifted version, also.

Step 2: Take your finished photographs to a copy center where you can make photocopies and enlarge them to your desired size. Black and white copies are okay.

Step 3: Outline your figure with a black marker or pen, following the outside contours of your body. These dark lines will help eliminate excess visual information and make it easier to see through your tracing paper.

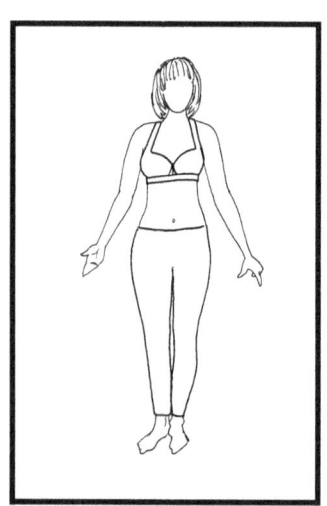

The pose does not have to be exotic. Make sure you hold your arms away from your body.

Step 4: Lay a piece of artist's tracing paper over your prepared photocopies. Trace your figure, following the dark marker lines.

Step 5: If you want your reference figures to be on more substantial paper, photocopy them onto thicker paper. Some designers like their reference figures on card stock to really stand up to handling.

Sources of Inspiration

Let the entire world be your inspiration! Keep your eyes open when shopping, vacationing, or even watching television. Great works of art can provide inspirational color schemes. A trip to the mall can give you trim, cut, and fabrication concepts. Simply taking a walk and looking at the homes and the flora and fauna of your environment can trigger ideas for design motifs. A small notebook stashed in a pocket or bag will allow you to write down concepts and ideas anywhere. To get you started looking for ideas, here is a list of sources that I have found useful for my own visual research:

Videos. There is a wealth of costume information available on videotape. From step-by-step instructional videos to star studded shows, a library of videos can be very inspirational. The benefit of video is that you get to see different costume styles in motion and from a variety of angles. Videos allow the designer to look at design details such as the way different lengths and configuration of fringe can move or how much freedom of movement a particular skirt provides.

Organize pictures you have torn from advertisements and magazines by filing them.

Magazines. There are several major national and regional Middle Eastern dance publications. Some clubs send out monthly or quarterly newsletters which feature articles and images of dancers. Fashion magazines, especially titles that focus on haute couture, can provide inspiration for materials, cuts, and surface design details that can be imported into the world of Middle Eastern costume design.

Festivals and Events. Attending a dance festival will allow you to see costumes for sale, costumes on dancers, and the numerous promotional materials to collect for your clip files or scrap books. These events are a feast for the eyes and can be an inspirational boon for the dancer. Take your sketchbook, a camera, and notebook to record design information.

Advertising. Many dancers put out promotional advertisements for events, products, and services. These flyers can be an excellent source of design information. Cull through and save only the ones that appeal to you the most. Look for clean, clear pictures that that inspire you and make sure to store them in a useful format such as in a scrapbook, binder, or files.

Web sites offer goods, advice, and services, but also lots of images to inspire and delight.

World Wide Web. There is a large and active community of dancers on the Internet. Taking a tour of the World Wide Web can provide you with lots of visual information. From monthly newsletters to virtual communities, mailing lists, and promotional sites for dancers and vendors, there is a tremendous variety in sites geared to the Middle Eastern dancer. There is a list of sites to get you started in the resources section.

Clip Book

One way to organize the images that inspire you is to keep a clip book. Sometimes called a clip file, idea book, or just a scrapbook, this is a collection of images that designers find inspiring. This can be as simple as a folder filled with pictures. Being organized will allow you to easily flip through your personal image bank when you are in need of inspiration. When you see something that inspires you—a post card, a picture in a magazine, photographs from an event, whatever it may be—make a copy or place the original in your clip book. Organize your book to suit your own creative needs with sections based on style, color, shapes, or garments type.

A clip book can be as simple as a notebook with images sketched and taped into it. Some dancers like to keep their visual information in a three-ring binder, mounted on paper, or slipped into protective plastic sleeves. Others like to use a scrapbook, making their clip book a creative assemblage of ideas that's fun to show off to other designers. If you like to draw, a sketchbook can be used in much the same way but the white color allows you to augment your image collection with your own sketches, ideas, and notes.

Portfolio

Many designers forget to keep track of their own process as a designer. Maintaining a portfolio can help you record your projects in a format that is fun to show off to friends and potential clients. Unlike a photographic brag book, which is an album of snap shots of your costumes, a portfolio is more formal and includes a variety of materials that show your process as a designer. Even if you never plan on being a professional designer, a portfolio is a great way to showcase your talents for yourself, family, and friends.

The Case

Begin by selecting a size and configuration for your portfolio. The portfolio can be as simple as a three-ring binder with slip-in page protectors. Artist's portfolios tend to be larger and have multi-ring pages, which can get quite expensive. Also, look in the business organization section of your favorite office supply store for high quality zipped binders, at a fraction of the cost. Even a basic black binder will work to get you started. You can always upgrade your case at a later time.

Images

The images become the most important feature of your portfolio. Instead of relying on standard-size snapshots, make enlargements. You don't have to go to a professional photographer to get good quality photos but you will get the best results if you make this investment. An alternative is to have a friend photograph you in front of a plain background, so as not to distract from the costume. Take lots of pictures because even if you shoot an entire roll of film, you may only wind up with two to five decent pictures. Also remember to take close-ups of details that you are especially proud of.

Make sure to date your costume illustration and include notes on fabrication and technique.

Oct 2000
Cold-shoulder body stocking

Drawings

Make photocopies of some of your finished sketches to include in your portfolio. If you place a concept sketch beside the finished garment, it will show the viewer your design process from concept to costume. If you are working on your drawing skills, you will probably want to show them off. Even if you aren't totally pleased with your sketches, including them in your portfolio shows your skill at being able to creatively visualize your projects.

Text

Make sure that your items are labeled. Costumes should, at the very least, be dated so the viewer can get an understanding of how your skills have progressed over time. If you design for dancers other than yourself, you should include the names of your clients or models in the photos. At the opening of your portfolio, you may want to include:

- An index which lists the costumes in the order they appear.
- A mission statement as a designer or even your design resume.
- Documentary information about the details of each costume.

Promotional Materials

If you are a professional designer, or dream of becoming one someday, the portfolio is one of the vital tools you will use to help develop clients. You will also need flyers, brochures, business cards, or other promotional materials. Having a place to store them in your portfolio will allow you to whip them out at a moment's notice. If you aren't planning on starting a business, you might want to keep promo materials for yourself as a performer, for troupes you might be involved in, or classes you might be teaching.

5 An Analytic Approach to Designing Bedlah

The process of design is all about finding solutions for design problems. Each step of the design process is a question that needs to be addressed by the designer. Each of these questions has an infinite number of possible answers. The designer must pick and choose which design elements to select to complete the finished garment. Consider the unique problems encountered when designing a costume that uses the standard bedlah format. Not only do you have to design a complete ensemble composed of many individual garments, but all of these parts must be integrated to create a unified and harmonious entirety.

Unlike the first few chapters of this book, this chapter will take an analytical approach to the process of designing the bra and belt set. I will be introducing the type of design questions that need answers in order to create a beautiful and functional bedlah set. Throughout this chapter I will be using the design terminology introduced in Chapter 3 to help describe the design process. As you answer these questions, images of costumes will begin to form in your mind. Designers articulate the answers to these questions through the use of notes and sketches, so get ready to draw!

Set Goals and Take Stock

Each dancer has her own unique set of needs and goals she wishes to achieve. The first step of the design process is to figure out what your particular needs are. Goals can be anything from physical attributes to feelings you want the costume to inspire in the viewer or yourself. This is a time to explore your needs and expectations. Take the time to sit down and develop a list of your own needs. Below is an example list to get you started thinking about your own goals.

My costume will:

Be suitable for performance at an event. Complement my figure. Highlight the movements of my hips. Be comfortable. Earn compliments. It will be red with roses. It will have a long flowing full skirt. It will cover my tummy but reveal my sides. I want to look taller and more elegant. Show off my spinning abilities.

When you are done, go back and look at your list.

As you review this list, you will notice that some of these needs are actually design features that can form a concrete starting point for designing. This short list establishes several major design features such as the color (red), a design motif (roses), and the shape of the skirt (long flowing and full). Your own brainstorming list should have some concrete concepts. If it's

Costume with unadorned bra.

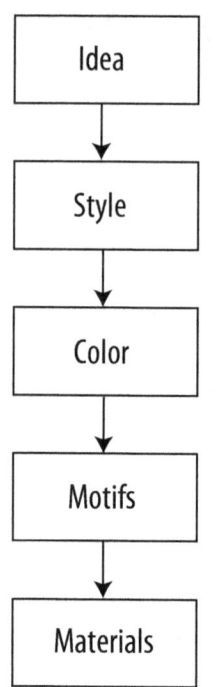

The initial steps down the analytic design process.

full of amorphous thoughts such as "I want a beautiful costume," go back and try again until you come up with more specific information. Here are a few design questions that can help you trigger more specific thoughts for this list.

- What parts of my figure do I want to emphasize?
- What style of costuming do I prefer?
- Which types of features did the last costume I loved have that made it special?
- What will I use this costume for?
- What colors move me? What looks good on me?
- Who's my favorite dancer? What do they wear?
- Which dancer has a similar figure? What do they wear?

As you begin answering these questions, you will find that more information about your desires and needs will come pouring forth. Some of these issues may trigger negative thoughts about your figure or your dance ability. But realize that dance is a journey and everyone is at a different space of development along their own paths. Don't compare yourself to others; rather, focus on making the best costume for your body and your dance style.

Designing Bedlah

While skirts and pants, vests and blouses can be coordinated, mixed and matched, the bra and belt needs to form a strong design unit. The design elements between these two pieces need to work together to create a unified whole even thought they are frequently separated by an expanse of skin. There are steps you can take that will instantly coordinate these two parts.

Choose a Style

While inspiration can strike like a bolt of lightening, there are times when you won't know where to begin. One of the first things a designer will do is select a style. There are many stylistic options listed in chapter three and images to inspire throughout this and other books. Selecting a style limits the palette of design elements. If your style, however, is high glamour beads and sequins, then you have to try to limit your design options even further.

Select Your Colors

There are many sources of inspiration for colors. Anything from a bouquet of flowers to a work of art can provide you with a color scheme for a costume. Revisit the section on color in Chapter 3 to find some approaches to developing an effective palette of colors. When contemplating your color schemes, make sure to take into consideration what materials are actually available in your area. A trip to your favorite fabric store can provide you with practical ideas, allowing you to base your color scheme on available fabrics and trims. But don't feel limited by the colors in your local stores. Many fabrics, such as cotton, rayon, linen, and silk can be effectively dyed at home.

Elegant costume made from simple supplies, ribbon, coins, and chainette fringe.

An Analytic Approach to Designing Bedlah

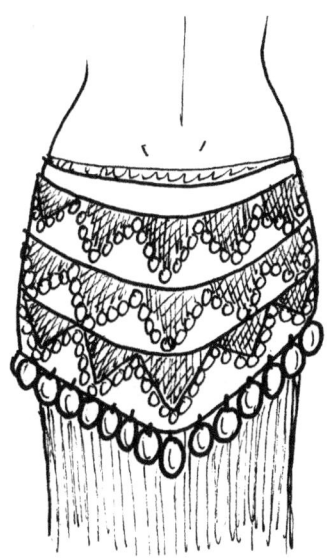

 If you have purchased a shimmy belt, you can use this technique to build a coordinating bra.

Develop a Design Motif

Selecting a motif for use throughout your costume will help to reduce the overwhelming number of options available. A motif can be a simple geometric shape repeated throughout your garment or it can be a complex representational pattern worked in beads and sequins. A motif can be ready-made, in the form of a beaded appliqué, a ribbon or braid, or even a design lifted from a piece of fabric. If you have trouble selecting a motif, try to find an image that you connect with. To instantly coordinate your bra and belt, use your selected design motif on both pieces.

Use the Same Materials

Using the same fabric, beads, and trim on both the bra and belt will create a unified look between the top and bottom. By simply using the same materials, you can begin to coordinate the costume. Try to use the same proportions of each different design element on both the top and bottom. For example, if you are using black as an accent, try to use the same amount of black on both pieces. Think of it as a percentage. The black should appear in the same quantities on both the bra and belt. If 20% of the design is black on the bra, then you should use the same percentage on the belt.

This technique can be an effective way to revive a costume where one piece has become separated from its mate. Take the piece to a local craft, fabric, or bead shop and attempt to match the materials used for the surface design. If you maintain the ratio of colors, materials, and motifs you might be able to manufacture a replacement garment. Even if the supplies are not an exact match, you can still revive the costume. This doesn't mean you have to exactly recreate the original piece. Instead, you can create something totally new and innovative that has the same look and feel.

Repeat the Design Lines

When you are designing the bra and belt, try to use the same types of design lines. For instance, if you are using angular lines on the bra, transfer these same angular designs to the belt. By using the principles of balance and repetition throughout the design of your bedlah, the costume pieces will naturally look like they belong together and will not appear disjointed or ungainly. Integrating the design lines along with repeated motifs will further help to integrate these two garments.

Design Problem: Fringe

While these suggestions and examples might seem obvious to you, the analytical approach can be applied to more specific design issues. In this next example, the position, placement, and style of fringe for a bra and belt is our design problem. To demonstrate how a question and answer approach can work for you, here are just a few of the key issues that determine the effectiveness of fringe placement.

Fringe works with the dancer's motion to amplify subtle movements. The placement, length, and style of the fringe is critical to the effectiveness of

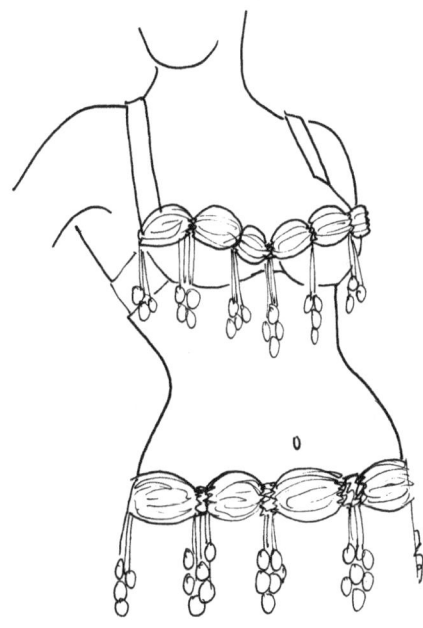

Repeating design lines.

the costume, not only for aesthetics, but also from a functional point of view. Here are just a few of the many questions you must ask yourself before you begin working with fringe:

- Do I want to use fringe on my costume?
- Do I want to use swags, strands, loops, or tassels?
- Do I want to use fringe to obscure any body parts? If so, which ones?
- What types of motions do I use most in my dance?
- Is there a feature that I want to highlight by using strategic fringe placement?

When it comes to fringe placement, the dance vocabulary of the performer should be taken into consideration and play a major role in determining the final look of the costume. Dance costumes should support your movements, accenting the movement and flow of your performance technique. The design process is about striking a balance, picking and choosing the areas of emphasis, and using the elements and principles of design to develop a beautiful ensemble. As you read the list of movements below, turn each into a design question. For instance, in the first section on shoulder movements, ask yourself these questions, inserting the location of choice in the blank:

- Do I want to emphasize my _____?
- What style of movements does my dance emphasize in my _____ region?
- Which portion of my figure should be emphasized the most?

Shoulder Movements

Our dance vocabulary is full of arm and shoulder articulations. While, traditionally, most of the design emphasis has been on the bust and hips, fringe can be effectively used at the shoulder to emphasize creative arm work.

Shoulder flicks and pops. Up and down motions will be accentuated by shoulder swags that are loose and hang from the bra straps across the top of the arm. Epaulettes with strand fringe will provide a lot of extra movement by emphasizing the shoulders and making articulations appear bigger.

Shimmies. Created by a forward and back motion, swinging strand fringe, either attached to suspended shoulder swag or an epaulette, will jump and sway to accentuate shoulder shimmies.

Arms over the head. If you swing your arms straight up and hold them over your head for extended periods of time, you might want to forgo shoulder swags. Swags can fall from the biceps region and can bunch unattractively on the shoulder. If you put your arms up for short periods of time, this isn't a problem, but for extended combinations, swags might not be the best option.

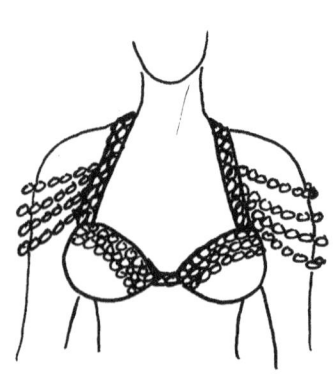

An Analytic Approach to Designing Bedlah

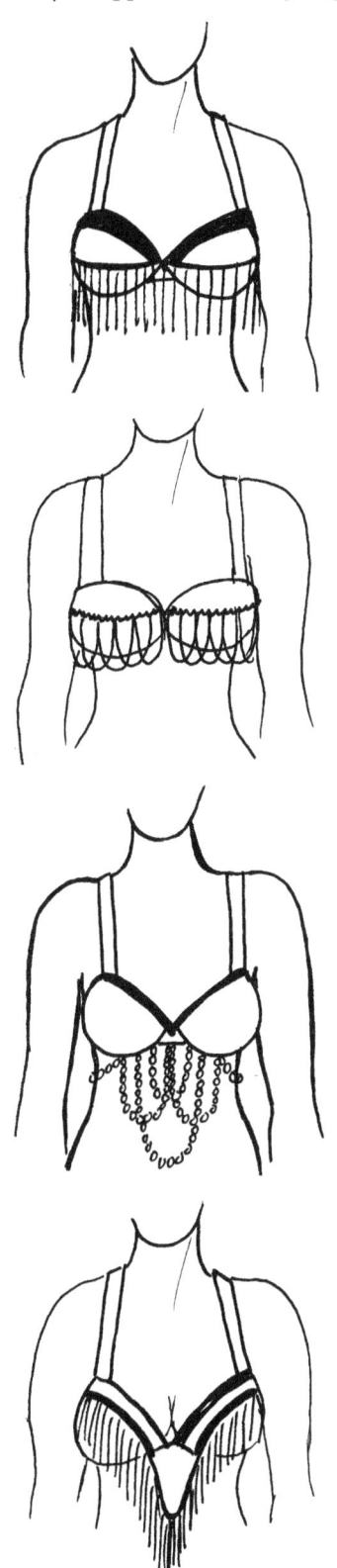

Chest Movements

Some dancers elect not to place fringe on their bras. There are many reasons for this decision ranging from having too ample a bosom to dancing in a style that doesn't rely heavily on isolated chest movements. Some dancers simply prefer to draw the viewer's eye downward to their hip region. Eliminating fringe from the bra while adding some to the hips will naturally focus attention exactly where the dancer wants it. However, many dancers like to accentuate their chest and fringe on the bra is an excellent way to achieve this effect.

Lifts and drops. Quick up and down motions can be effectively accentuated by any suspended design elements. Swag fringe has a tendency to swing outward from the body and is particularly effective for these types of movements. Strand or looped fringe will create a radiating spray of movement with this type of motion.

Shimmies. The best way to accentuate shimmies is with strand fringe, which will move in any direction and is especially responsive to quick flicks. The longer the fringe the bigger the shimmies need to be to make them respond.

Circles and undulating motions. Swag fringe will sway front to back and is especially effective at highlighting undulations. Chest circles can make strand fringe bounce up and down or sway, depending upon the speed of the movement.

Belly Movements

Some dancers like to hide their tummies under a wall of fringe. Other dancers want to leave their torsos uncluttered. There are dancers in the middle of these two extremes who carefully plan their costumes, with a sweep of fringe that adds visual interest without concealing movements.

Rolls and torso undulations. Use fringe or swags made from small seed beads suspended from the bottom edge of the bra so it will rest against the body to emphasize body rolls and waves. A centralized swag or drop of fringe down across the midriff will catch the light and accentuate the motions. Swags will give peeks of the body below, while fringe can make a concealing curtain that will still move and sparkle.

Flutters. If your flutters are particularly strong, swags can be very effective, especially if your muscle control can cause them to bounce off the body. Keep the beads lightweight and small in scale. Flutters can quickly be obscured under heavy curtains of fringe. If you perform flutters, keep your fringe short and mounted high on the bra.

Hip Movements

The core of a Middle Eastern dancer's repertoire of movements are precision isolation and articulation of the hips. To accentuate hip movements, consider which movements dominant your repertoire. Some dancers twist more; some rely heavily on up-down motions. If you have a set of hip motions that play a bigger role in your performance style, then designing your costume to emphasize them can add zing and life to your ensemble.

Lifts and drops. Swags are particularly effective for accenting lifts and drops. They will swing forward away from the body during sharp lift and drop combinations and can be integrated into design layouts with strand fringe.

Twisting motions. Strand and looped fringe will respond well to twisting motions, shifting out and away from the body in smooth arcs, especially when placed around the hips. Fringe positioned centrally in the front of the body tends to move less than fringe on the rear or sides of the belt.

Shimmies. Strand fringe and close looping fringe will react to shimmies with the most life and jump. Longer strands take more work to really move than shorter lengths. Lightweight plastic beads will bounce and jump more erratically than heavier glass beads. Thick Egyptian fringe will create a blur of beads during intense shimmies.

Ultimately, well-placed fringe requires knowing which movements and body parts that you want to emphasize. If you coat every edge of your costume with fringe, you could loose your focal point. The viewer needs to have guides to pull their eyes around a costume. A wall of fringe will not have spaces for the eyes to rest. In addition, a fringe-coated costume will be in nearly constant motion, so isolations need to be extremely precise, for without stillness to counterbalance movement, distinctive steps will meld and fuse into each other.

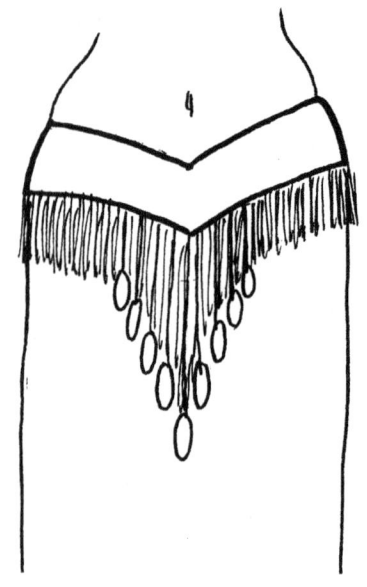

Accenting shimmies and twisting moves.

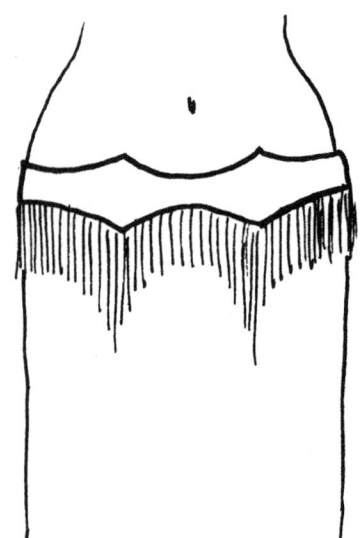

Strand fringe can follow the shape of the belt and, if kept short, is fairly easy to move.

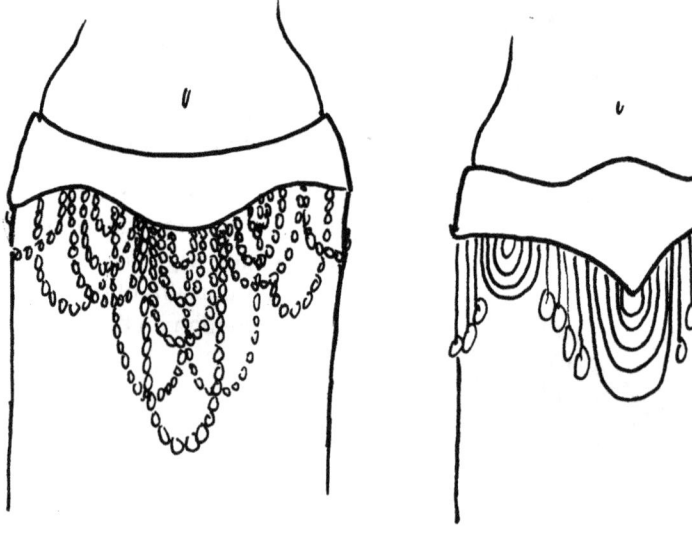

Center and right: Swags are good for lifts and drops.

6 Designing for Every Body

No matter what size you are, from 2 to 22, there is a flattering costume out there waiting for you to design or buy. There are numerous books on the shelves of bookstores designed to give you practical advice for putting together attractive functional wardrobes that make you look the best you possibly can. But the list of books available for the Middle Eastern dance costumer is pretty short! Each designer, teacher, dancer, costume maker, and seamstress will have their own approaches, not only for design and construction, but also for aesthetics. But everyone can agree that there are three basic issues that all costumes must address.

- Is the costume beautifully constructed and designed?
- Does it fit?
- Does it look good on you?

This last question has as much to do with your individual figure traits as it does with your performance technique and personal style. In this section, I will discuss my methods for body analysis, evaluation, and subsequent design choices.

My approach is one of balance. There are no do's and don'ts in my design book, but rather a series of choices you will make about you or your client's figure. Consequently, this chapter is broken into two parts. First, I will present my favorite method for body analysis. It's fast, easy, and only requires a photograph. In the second part, I will present a list of features and ways to either emphasize or de-emphasize the body through the manipulation of the principles and elements of design. That way you, with the mind of a designer, can make informed creative decisions to create the best costume to suit your needs.

Body Analysis

There is no way to be impartial about your own figure. Imagery and a host of social messages concerning the body have bombarded everyone living in the Western world. The entertainment media has decided what is fashionable, acceptable, and desirable. I have met many a dancer so concerned about her figure that she became incapable of making decisions when it came to her own costume.

What costume is best? It's an eternal struggle to find something that not only looks good and fits well, but also falls into the budget. In this section, we will talk about the types of features that can enhance specific styles of bodies. The goal of a good costume is to play up your best features to their ultimate advantage. I encourage you to go into this process with an open mind and focus on the positive during this analysis.

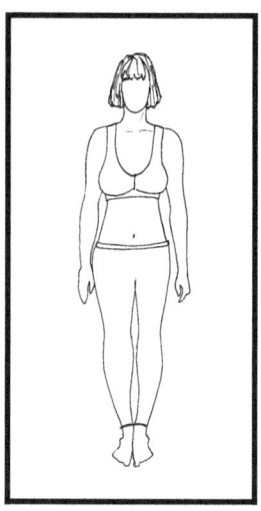

Step 1: Take your picture.

Step 1: Photograph your figure. Probably the most difficult part of this project is having a good, clean photograph taken. It needs to be full length. Be sure to wear a close-fitting garment such as a unitard, leotard, bathing suit, or underwear. You do not want to obscure the contours of your body. You may want to tie a contrasting ribbon around your waist to make marking the photo later easier.

Step 2: Enlarge the photo. Make the picture large enough to be easy to work with. This can be done a variety of ways. You could make a photo enlargement, photocopy the image using a copier's enlargement feature, or scan the picture into a computer and print out a larger copy. If none of these techniques are available to you, can just use the photo as it is; it will just be a little more difficult to see the results.

Step 3: Mark the key points. Using a black marker, put a large dot at the outside edge of each shoulder, at the waist, and at the hips.

Step 4: Connect the dots. Use a ruler or straight edge to connect the dots. Connect the shoulders with a straight line. Likewise for the hips. Now draw a straight line from the shoulder dot to the waist dot and then continue drawing down to the hip line. Repeat this process on the other side.

You will wind up with a boxy diagram of your body. This schematic will make it easy to see the formal organization of your body contours.

Dominant Body Shapes

The female human body is composed of a tremendous number of curves. We curve front to back, top to bottom, and side to side. Reducing your figure to a schematic serves only as a guideline for getting in touch with the core dynamic of your figure. There are many different systems for body analysis. When all is said and done, they vary in the details and terminology. So if you are already familiar with the "HOAX" system, or prefer to refer to bodies in terms of fruit, such as "apples" and "pears," there is no reason to abandon your system. Simply look for the similarities and apply them to your already developed system of body analysis.

My method is based on a comparison of the figure with basic geometric shapes. Females can be grouped into five basic shapes: **triangle, inverted triangle, rectangle, double triangle,** and **oval.**

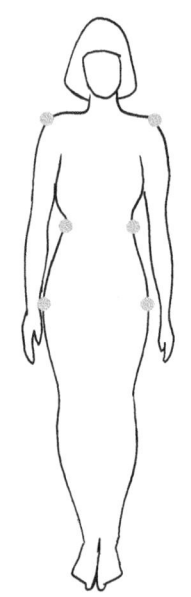

Step 3: Mark the key points.

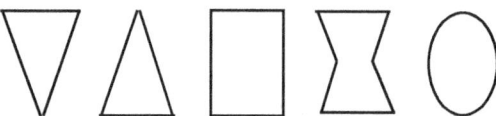

The design of the costume can either emphasize the shape of the figure or de-emphasize it. Some dancers like to play up their body type, while others like to camouflage the lines of their figures. In either case, the listings below offer suggestions to help you achieve the results that are right for you.

Designing for Every Body

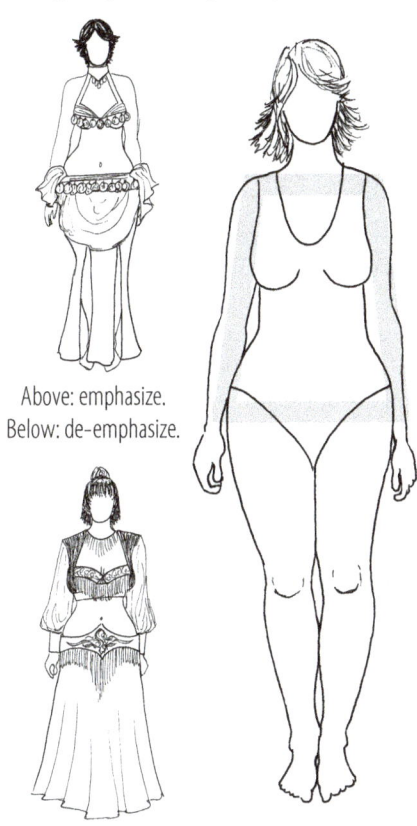

Above: emphasize.
Below: de-emphasize.

Triangle

If the hip line is longer than the shoulder line, you probably fall into this category. This is perhaps the most common body shape for women worldwide. Due to our role as mothers, our hips are generally wider to accommodate the birthing process.

To emphasize: Strong horizontal lines across the hips will emphasize the triangular figure shape. Adding additional hip poufs, scarves, and tucked veils will further broaden the figure. Wearing decorative cuffs that line up with the belt will extend the visual line past the hips. Fringe of a uniform length mounted around the hips from the bottom edge of the belt will emphasize the width of the hips. Pulling skirts up and tucking them into the belt will visually further extend the hips by drawing swooping lines up from the hem.

To de-emphasize: There are two approaches to minimizing the hip region. The first is to draw attention upward by playing up the chest and shoulders with strong design elements, well-placed focal points, and more elaborate decoration. The second is to address the needs of the hip itself. Avoid straight lines. Contour the upper and lower edges of the belt, making your belt wider at the center and narrower on the sides. Draw style-lines inward to the center of the body and drop long fringe at the center to create vertical lines down the middle of the body to draw the eye up and down, rather than across.

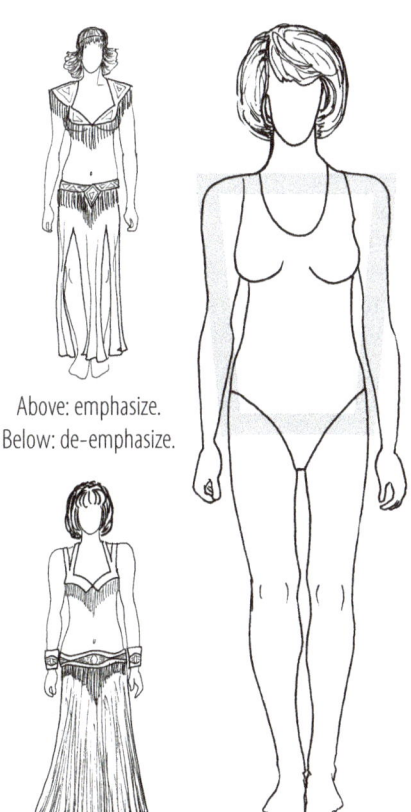

Above: emphasize.
Below: de-emphasize.

Inverted Triangle

A less common figure type is the inverted triangle, where the shoulder is wider than the hips. This body style can look very Amazonian and powerful. Narrow hips are also currently in style in the world of high fashion and many models of the last ten years have this body style.

To emphasize: First, read the de-emphasis list for the hourglass figure. In addition to those suggestions, play up the shoulder region with swags, decorative epaulettes, and cold shoulder styles of dresses with decorative trim at the cutouts. Narrow shoulder straps will give the visual appearance of more territory, especially with faux-halter styles such as the Y-back or collar styles. Putting more elaborate decoration on the bra than on the hips will instantly draw attention upwards. Emphasizing the "V" shape of the neckline will also draw attention outwards from the center of the bra to the shoulders.

To de-emphasize: To create visual balance for broad shoulders, expand the hip region. Look at the emphasis section of the triangular figure for a few ideas. Pull the eye down to the hip region with long centrally located fringe that hangs down center front of the bra, creating a line for the eye to follow downward to the belt. Use a balanced repeated design around the hips to draw the eye across the body. A pair of focal points, spread widely on the belt, will pull the eye outward. In dresses, look for styles that are fitted through the torso and don't pouf over the hips, which will invariably make the hips look narrower.

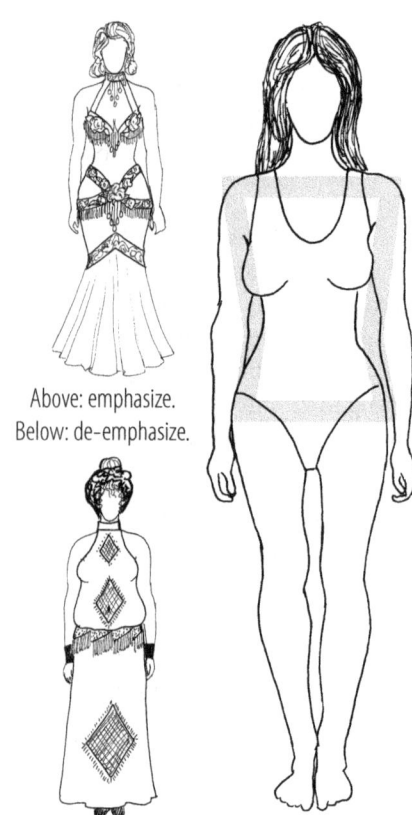

Above: emphasize.
Below: de-emphasize.

Double Triangle or Hourglass

When the shoulders and hips are balanced and the waist is narrower, you have an hourglass figure. Long viewed by many as the most "ideal" figure type, the hourglass figure is easy to costume due to the similar proportions of the top and bottom of the torso.

To emphasize: In this figure type, emphasizing a narrow waist is the focus of most of the design work. "V" shaped fringe hanging from the bra will form a visual arrow that points downward to the waist region. Avoid long, wide, or heavy belly drapes that can obscure the shape of the figure. Wearing a delicate belly chain can draw attention to this area, especially if the dancer can maneuver it during torso undulations. In dresses, elegant cutouts at the side of the body will emphasize the narrow waist, as will decorative lines that slide at an angle down the body.

To de-emphasize: Although it seems unlikely that a dancer would want to de-emphasize this body shape, it might be a necessity when performing with a troupe and a more uniform look is required. Soft draped tunics or beladi dresses will obscure the contours of the body. Heavy fringe hung from the bottom of the bra that wraps around to the back could also camouflage the region under a curtain of beads. Loose belly drapes that extend from the bra to the belt and belts that reach up to the waist with horizontal straps will also help to downplay the narrow waistline.

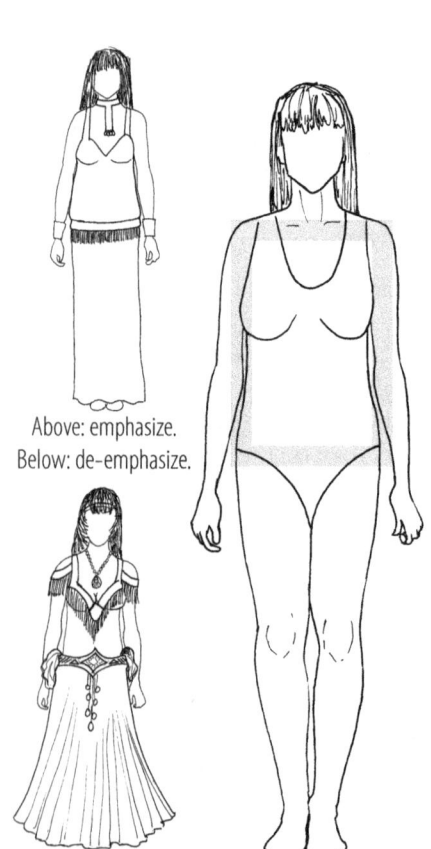

Above: emphasize.
Below: de-emphasize.

Rectangular

If the shoulders, hips, and waist are roughly the same width, you have the rectangular figure type. While at first glance you may feel discouraged, this figure style is the easiest to transform through the use of a carefully cut and well-fitted costume. Just remember that you can always build up both the bra and belt to help create the illusion of a more hourglass-like figure.

To emphasize: Look at the list of de-emphasizing ideas for the hourglass figure type. To emphasize this figure, wear little or no fringe on the bra and belt. This will produce less visual interest and movement. Instead, use color in bright hues that contrast with your skin to draw attention to your vertical shape. When fringe is used, dangling it down the center of the bra and the center of the belt will create a strong vertical axis that will draw the eye up and down the body. Square-cut belts with straight edges will emphasize the body by creating strong right angles.

To de-emphasize: If you want to minimize the strong vertical lines of your figure, add curves to the costume. Softly waving, shaped belt edges with fringe placed around the body is one good look for the rectangular figure. Another option is to break the strong lines of the figure with asymmetrically placed focal points and design features on both the bra and belt. Straps that connect the bra and belt and draw soft curves around the torso will keep the eye moving. Fitted dresses with oval cutouts, color blocking with curvy shapes of contrasting cloth, and skirts that flare at the ankle will all help add softly undulating lines. Alternatively, a loose shimmy dress, beladi dress, or gown that skims over the torso, but has emphasis at the shoulder and hip, can help create the illusion of a sculpted waistline.

Designing for Every Body

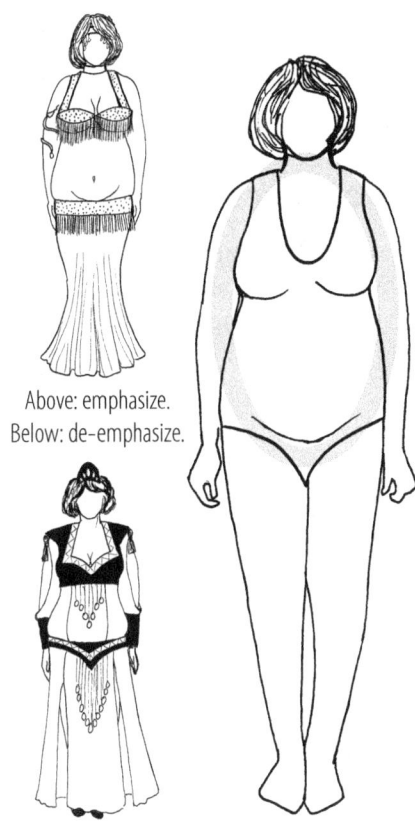

Above: emphasize.
Below: de-emphasize.

Oval

An oval figure is one where the shoulders and hips are relatively narrow and the waist is slightly wider. Pregnant women and women of size might find themselves in this group and their first instinct may be to conceal the belly region under a layer of cloth. But even dancers with this challenging figure type have options.

To emphasize: Wearing a two-piece bra and belt set with no fringe, stomach drapes, or tummy covers will emphasize this figure type. Wearing a belt low across the hips so the belly extends above it will draw attention to this area. Applying glitter to the belly, especially to a round fecund pregnant tummy, can effectively draw the eye to this feature and make it a focal point.

To de-emphasize: The most obvious method to de-emphasize this region is by wearing a gown. No matter if you choose a loose and flowing garment or a sleek fitted dress, the key issue is that the garment fits well. Too loose, and your movements will get lost in the fabric and folks will wonder what you are trying to hide. Too tight, and your dress will emphasize rather than conceal. Dancers committed to a bedlah style costume might want to consider the use of a decorative leotard, a stretch torso cover, or body stocking. These come in a variety of materials or can be custom made to match your costume. Careful fringe placement can also conceal the body; long fringe suspended from the lower edge of the bra can give peeks at this area during movements, but in general obscure the view. Veils and scarves can also be worn tucked into the bra and belt for a loose, draping, and inexpensive cover-up.

Height

Another issue that dancers are up against is height. Most ready made costumes are designed to fit an average range, but dancers over 5'8" (1.7 m) or under 5'4" (1.6 m) might find themselves faced with limited options for purchasing a well crafted, beautifully fit costume.

Shorter Frame

The petite dancer can quickly find herself overwhelmed by fringe. The goal is to draw long, lean lines with the surface decoration and use the fringe as further support. Keep the longer fringe to the center-front and -back of the belt only. Too much long fringe around the belt will visually weigh the dancer down. Long fringe on the bra can cover too much of the torso, obscuring dance motions and chopping up the dancer's figure. Keep the fringe short or use shaped fringe that is only long in specific places for emphasis.

A petite dancer should also consider the proportion of her figure and the thickness of her belt. A narrow belt will be more in proportion with the overall figure. Consider, too, the thickness of the bra straps. Thicker straps can look wider proportionally, giving the costume a heavy quality.

Taller Frame

Taller dancers have the opposite problems as petite dancers. Some narrow belts will seem insufficient and unsupportive. Even though it might be well-fitted and sturdy, if the belt is too small proportionally, it will look flimsy.

 Use lines to draw the eye up and down the body. Strong verticals and repeated color, from skirt to bra to headdress, will pull the viewer's gaze around your figure.

Narrow bra straps can give the impression of lingerie rather than of a finished costume. Long vertical lines in the design and placement of fringe will emphasize the height, and if the torso is long, a six-inch (15 cm) wash of beads can look beautiful without obscuring the torso.

Working With Individual Features

Some dancers find that they want to play up or de-emphasize one or more dominant features. Explore the illustrations on the next several pages to find some suggestions for working with specific prominent features. This simple list of design features will give you some ideas for ways of building flattering designs into your costume.

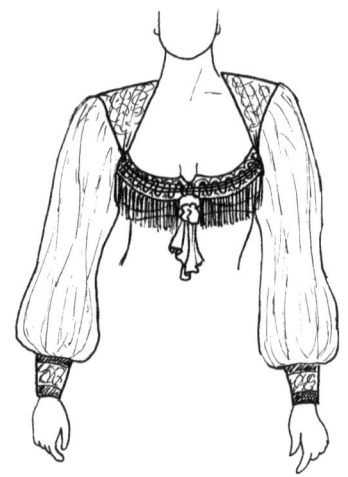

A loose blouse with built-up shoulders can balance wide hips.

Neck

To emphasize: Use thin, elegant chokers, beautiful jewelry, bras with collar shaped straps, and Y-shaped bra straps that draw the line from the bra up towards the neck. Vests with shaped keyhole-style vests will also keep attention around a long, elegant neck.

To de-emphasize: Wide chokers with dangling elements that reach down across the chest will at once conceal the neck while drawing attention down and away. Wearing a veil around the neck and allowing it to hang down the back will cover the neck region and draw the eye elsewhere. Dresses and vests with standing collars are another option that can conceal this region.

Shoulders

To emphasize: Frame with design features like shoulder swags, epaulettes, choli, and dresses with shoulder cut outs. Gypsy-styled blouses worn off the shoulder with a vest or bedlah decorated with large design motifs at the top of the bra cups will draw the eyes outward to the shoulders. Decorating the arms with biceps jewelry or short sleeve puffs worn high on the arm will draw attention up the arm to the shoulder.

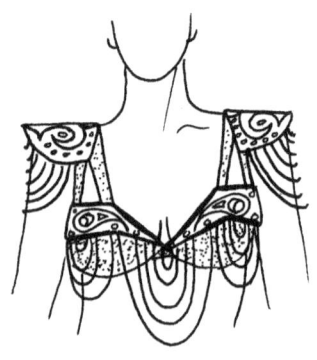

Epaullettes can visually extend the shoulder line to balance wide hips.

To de-emphasize: Draw the attention of the viewer to the center of the bra by using strong centrally located decorative motifs with long, decorative swags and drops to pull the eye to the middle of the body. Wearing a well-fitted vest with sheer sleeves can conceal this area beautifully by gracefully skimming over the shoulder region. Dresses with shoulder pads can help build up an overly sloped or rounded shoulder line.

Bustline

To emphasize: Use lots of fringe. Cover the bra in a bright, contrasting design. Design the bra so that it has bigger cups than you might need to create the illusion of a larger or fuller bust. Use tricks such as padding or tilting the cups to create more cleavage. Use narrow straps to emphasize the size of the cups and don't overly decorate the straps. Use circular surface design elements that follow the curve of the bra and hang fringe from the apex of the bust, maximizing the amount of swing.

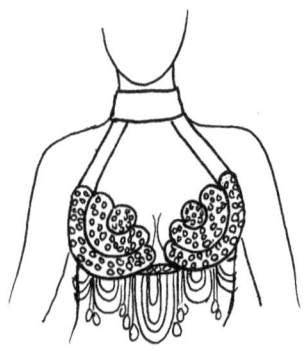

Rhinestone-encrusted bra with swags accentuates the bust.

Designing for Every Body

Emphasize the hips to de-emphasize the bust.

To de-emphasize: Avoid excessive fringe. Let fringe hang from the bottom edge of the bra, causing it to lie against the body. Use swags instead of strand or narrow looped fringe, which move less. Put decorative design treatments above the apex of the bust only, leaving the underside of the bra cups plainer. Make sure that the bra you select to use for your base is both sturdy and well-fitted, giving you ample coverage and support.

Arms

To emphasize: Wear long, closely-fitted sleeves, opera length gloves, or jewelry that accents to draw the eye from wrist to biceps. Arm poufs made from soft, drapey fabric with slits that gracefully swag from shoulder to wrist reveal the arms and frame their shape, especially when they are extended.

To de-emphasize: Arm poufs and loosely-fitted sleeves will cover the arms and conceal them from view. Dresses and choli with full-length sleeves will conceal the arm. Wearing short cuffs will draw the viewer's attention to the hands, as will sparkly jewelry at the wrists and fingers.

Midriff and Abdomen

To emphasize: Leave bare and exposed to show it off. Frame it with short fringe from the bust and an elegant belt line that points upwards towards the midriff area. French cut straps worn over the hips will also draw the eye up to the waist, emphasizing its shape. Wear dresses with sexy cutouts that follow the contours of the body. Belly chains, jewelry worn as stomach drapes, and swags of beads that pull the eye in to the center of the body will all draw attention to this area.

To de-emphasize: Torso covers, belly drapes, long concealing fringe, and loose flowing dresses that skim without clinging are all garments that can help draw attention away from this area. Long decorative drapes that part to give peeks of the torso are a way of covering without totally obliterating the body. Loose dresses, cut low down the middle, can show off a slice of the midriff while covering the torso.

Emphasizing your midriff and arms.

Hips

To emphasize: Use strong horizontal lines, lots of long beading, and high contrasting motifs to draw attention away from the center and out towards the hip region. Wider, thicker, and substantial belts will also add visual weight and pull the eye down. Keeping the bra simple in line and surface embellishments, while building up the belt as the key focal point, will further emphasize the hips.

To de-emphasize: Draw attention towards the center of the body axis by using long narrow stomach drapes, belt styles that curve either up or down at the center, and belts that are thicker and more substantial in the middle than at the sides. Avoid wearing cuffs that are made of the same materials as the belt. This will give the visual appearance of a further extended hip line. Wear skirts that have fuller hems and that sweep gracefully from the hipline to the floor.

Legs

To emphasize: Tight skirts with deep flounces, long slits up to the thigh or hip, or skirts that have revealing decorative seam treatments will all emphasize the leg. The "classic" skirt with two openings, when worn with the panels pushed back to reveal the thighs, will draw attention down from the torso to the your legs.

To de-emphasize: Wear pants without slits in opaque cloth. Wear closed skirts or, if the skirt has slits, wear narrow pants below. Sarong-style skirts will only put one leg on view if you have one that you want to showcase.

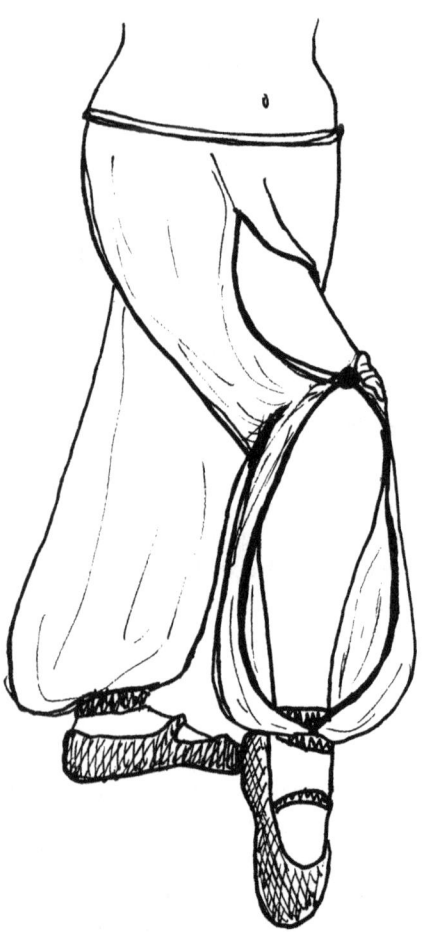

Emphasizing the legs.

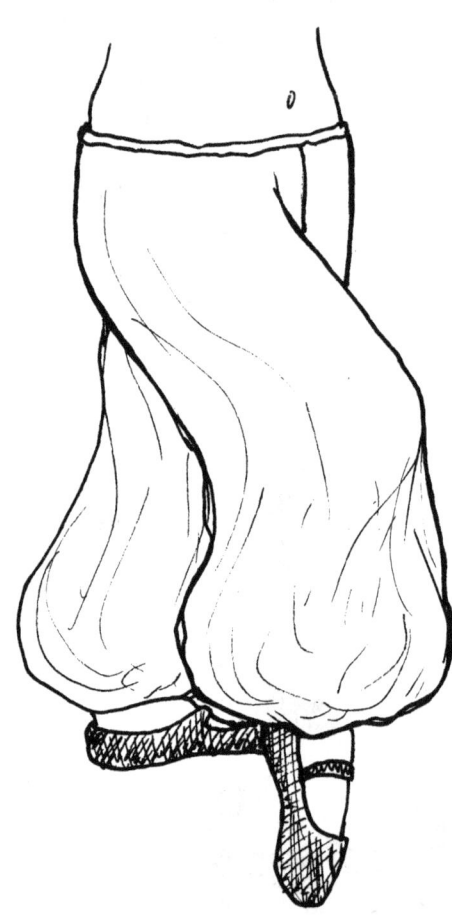

De-emphasis.

Part II
Bedlah Construction and Embellishment

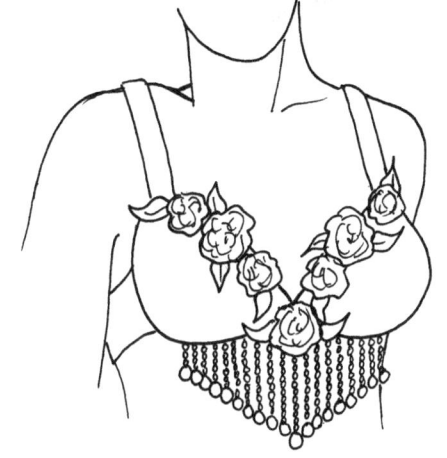

The nuts and bolts of creating a bra and belt set are covered here in Part II. While Part I presented a theoretical approach to design, here we introduce the hands-on techniques for building the bra and belt set from the ground up. From selecting materials and supplies to fitting the final garment, the chapters in this section step the reader through the process of construction and embellishment of bedlah.

Chapters 7 and 8 present the key issues in building the foundations for the bra and belt. Chapter 9 introduces the most popular beads, sequins, spangles, and jewels used to decorate the surface of dance wear. The next chapter goes over the basic beading techniques from flat beading to building custom fringe. In Chapter 11, one approach to developing designs from clip art is presented along with illustrations of each step.

Every seamstress has a basket of tricks and techniques she uses to construct costumes. This is only one approach to making a set of bedlah. Keep your mind open to ideas and ask the experts in your area for advice as you work to build your costumes. Pick and choose the techniques that work best for you, use them, and refine them as you develop your sewing and beading skills. There is no one "right way" to get the job done. And remember, creativity and skill can stretch a budget. Elegant, well-made costumes don't have to cost a fortune.

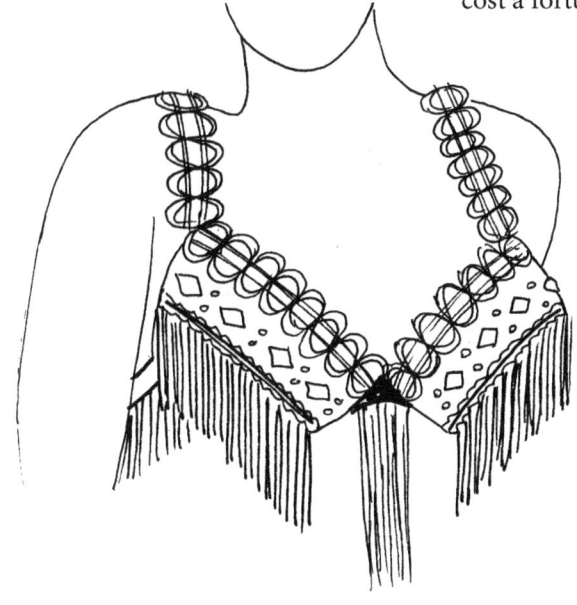

Bra Cup Magic — Four Steps to Enhance Cleavage

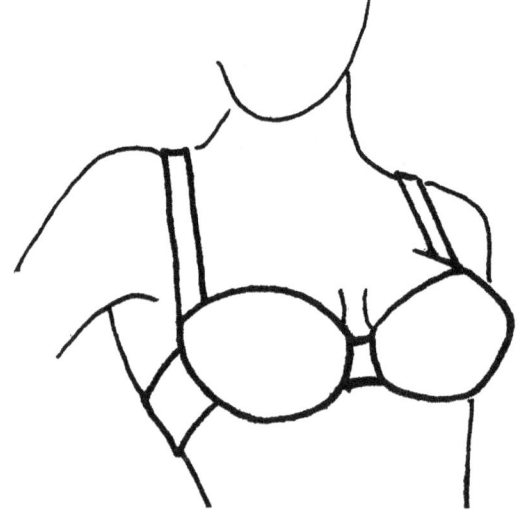

Fit

Buy a bra that has stable, sturdy cups, fits well, and looks good.

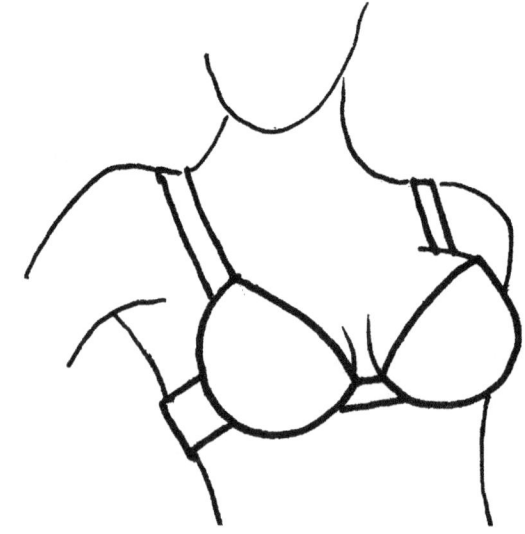

Tilt

Deconstruct the bra and tilt the cups. This provides lateral support.

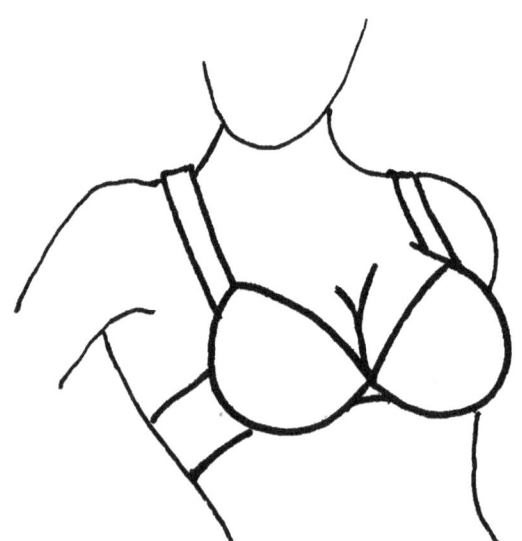

Squeeze

Bring the underwires together, pushing the bust together from the side.

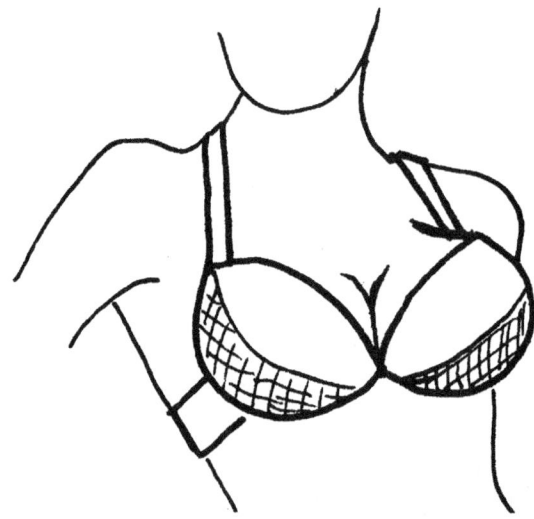

Pad

Add padding to the bra to lift the bust further. For less amply-endowed dancers, using the next larger cup size and padding it to create cleavage will give the illusion of a fuller bust.

7 Bra Construction

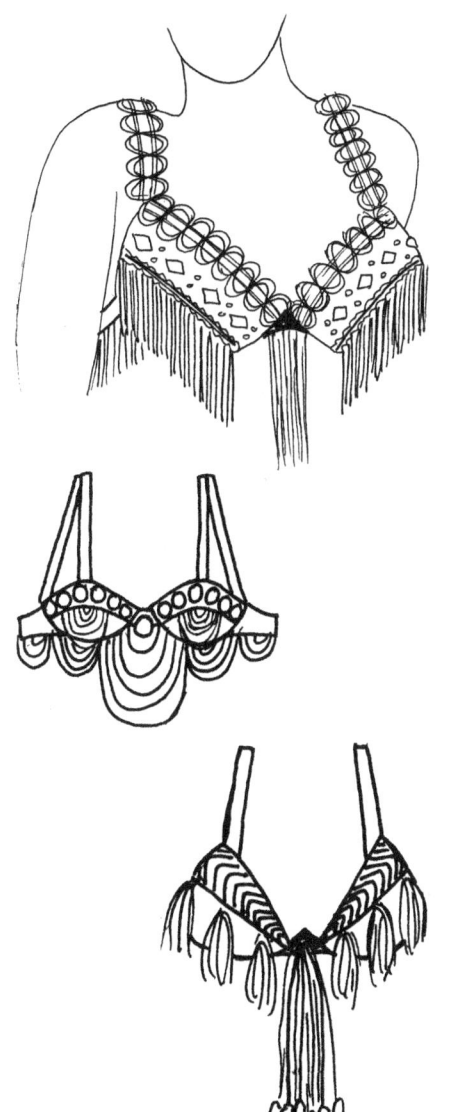

A bra is, without a doubt, one of the most complex garments that a woman wears. Some bras are made with as many as thirty different pieces to help shape, lift, and control the bustline. Finding a bra that fits can be frustrating experience. When you finally find the perfect bra, you have to stock up because styles change with the season. Even more challenging is finding the perfect bra to serve as a base for belly dance costuming, due to the limited numbers of suitable styles. In this chapter, I will be going over the bra making process from shopping to shapingand from deconstruction to decoration.

Buying a Bra

The most common method for constructing a costume bra is to build from a lingerie bra base. There are a few features that need to be present for the bra to make a good candidate for transforming into a performance piece. Where does one begin? With so many bras styles available on the retail market today, it is important to narrow down the materials and construction features that will provide the best support for both the dancer's body and the embellishments. Look for the following characteristics.

Firmly woven. You do not want your bra base to stretch. When you put it on, it should shape you. The bra should remain firm when you move and bend. Remember, the cups have to do double duty, supporting both you and the decorations.

Padded. Bras that have light to heavy padding will provide the dancer with a firm base upon which to stitch the surface decorations, especially fringe. Padded bras have the additional benefit of having more built in shaping and internal structure that will help to create a beautiful cleavage line.

Full coverage. There are many styles of bras that are firmly woven and lightly padded but which do not provide ample coverage. For instance, demi-bras may barely cover the nipple region on some dancers while others might find them the perfect amount of coverage. Since most bras are intended not to be seen except in private, they are not designed with our needs as dance costumers in mind. Every bra style is different, so don't shy away from demi-bras completely. But when you try the bra on, ask yourself "Would I want to go out of the house this exposed?"

Underwires. Bras are engineered to support and shape the bustline. Underwires serve as a supporting base for the cantilevering effect of the bra cups. While you might think the straps control the lift of the bust, in reality it's the underwires and chest band that keep the bra in place and provide the structure. Make sure that the underwires don't dig into the side of your bust mound. This is an indication that the wire width is too narrow for your needs.

In addition, not all cup sizes are created equal. Your 36B might be wider than the wire will support, requiring a step up. If the wire is poking into your arm, it's too wide and you might want to look for a different style or manufacturer.

Popular Bra Styles

No matter what store you frequent or brand you favor, there are only a few styles that are best suited for to withstand the transformation into a costume piece.

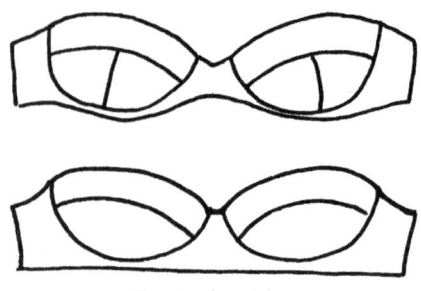

Two strapless styles.

Strapless. These bras make an excellent base for belly dance costumes. Strapless bras tend to have good bust coverage and a very stable base. However, the shape of the cups is very horizontal. Strapless bras are available in larger sizes than push-up bras. Amply endowed dancers should explore the strapless as an option. Look for a two-piece or three-piece construction, which is more supportive and sturdier. This is a good style to select if you like vintage shaping to your costume.

Push-up. This is a popular style and available from a wide variety of companies. The push-up bra uses careful shaping, contouring of the padding, and placement of the cups to achieve a bust-enhancing decolage. Push-up bras are the bra of choice for most dancers and are currently available in a wide range of colors and fabrications.

Push-up bra.

Demi-bra. Designed to lift the bust from below while leaving the top of the bust uncovered, the demi-bra acts much like a shelf. These cups tend to be smaller, top to bottom, than other styles of bras. Because they offer less coverage, some styles of demi-bra are too revealing for performance wear.

Molded bra. These bras are made from poly-fiber or foam that's been formed and molded into the shape of the bra. There are no darts or seaming on these bras, giving them a smooth shape and fit under garments such as sweaters and T-shirts. Because they are made from shaped padding, they provide enough thickness to support surface decoration. However, make sure that the molded bra you purchase not only fits well, but also has underwires to provide enough support. Voluptuous dancers may be able to find this style in larger cup styles at specialty stores.

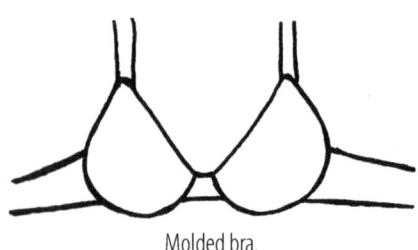

Molded bra.

Bra Sizes

Sizing is a big mystery for most women. There is no one standard sizing method in the bra industry, and Europe and Australia use totally different systems. Sizes vary wildly and some brands even have their own sizing systems. In general, you take your under-bust measurement and add 4 or 5 inches, rounding to the nearest whole number. That's your band size. Your cup size is the determined by the difference between the band measurement and the measurement of the fullest part of your bust.

Not all bras are created equally. Some cups will fit and others will seem to big, too wide, or too narrow. Why is that? Not only is there is no industry standard for bra sizes, the industry participates in what is commonly called "vanity sizing" in which more expensive bras have smaller band sizes and larger cup sizes. So a woman who wears a 40C in a regular department store bra, might wear a 38D in a specialty store bra, making her feel both slimmer and more stacked.

Measuring your band and cup size.

Bra Construction

Difference	Cup Size
1"	A
2"	B
3"	C
4"	D
5"	DD
6"	F
7"	G/FF
8"	H

 The goal is to have a bra that looks like a costume piece, not an undergarment!

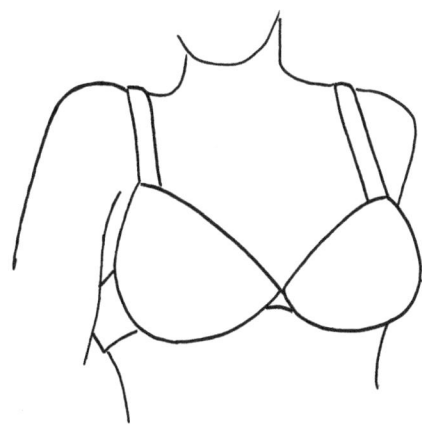

This illustration can be enlarged and used to draw samples.

When you find a style that fits, is comfortable, and works well as a dance bra base, buy as many of them as you can afford. Stockpile for future costumes to ensure that next time you have a great design in mind, you don't have to fruitlessly search for bras. You'll be able to simply reach into your stash and be ready to start. Also, if you have a model, brand, or style line that you are particularly fond of, watch for sales. Lingerie goes on sale in deep discounts after the winter holidays, around Valentine's Day, and during the back-to-school sales.

Using the Bra As-Is

Some dancers prefer not to deconstruct their bra. Rather, they like to use the bra as a readymade base. If you are planning on using the bra as-is by merely covering the cups and straps and decorating it, you might want to do a little planning ahead. Make sure that you have selected a bra that's as perfect as possible to do the job.

Wide, supportive straps will hold not only you, but the decoration as well. Some very beautiful bras that make lovely cleavage have skinny little straps. Look for bras that have enough support over the shoulder. Swapping out too-narrow straps in exchange for grosgrain ribbon is pretty easy, and can be done by hand or with a sewing machine.

Make sure the shape of the cups works for you, providing enough coverage and an attractive cleavage line. Since you will not be altering the position or shape of the cups, you want it to fit perfectly as is. When bra shopping, make sure to take along an assortment of bra pads if you are interested in developing cleavage. While you are shopping, try out a few moves in the fitting room, especially shimmies, shoulder rolls, and torso undulations that put the most stress on the bra.

Plan your surface decoration to accommodate existing straps. Fit the bra and stitch down the straps so they won't continue to slide. Tubes of cloth wrapped around the straps and hand stitched closed will hide the lingerie straps. Alternately, you can stitch on a wider decorative braid, ribbon, or trim to hide the structural elements.

Deconstruction

Wearing lingerie bra as a costume piece can be scary for some dancers. Most bras are designed to disappear under clothing. In addition, push-up or strapless bras are not designed for the amount of physical stress a dancer applies to the garment. The costume bra needs to provide support, security, and coverage. Costume straps need to be sturdier than their lingerie counterpart, with no slides to allow the cups to slide down the body. The chest band is usual wider or, in some cases, thinner but with much less give so that it hugs the chest firmly to prevent the bust from moving. Making the improvements to a lingerie bra requires taking it apart and reconstructing it from the cups up.

One-inch wide gros-grain ribbon will make excellent straps. It doesn't stretch and comes in hundreds of colors.

Step 1: Remove the bra straps, cutting as close to the cup as possible. Depending on the construction method, the bra strap can be unstitched and removed if it's applied to the surface of the cup.

Step 2: Remove the bra band. Snip as close as you can to the underwire if you are planning on tilting or moving the cups. If you want to retain the cups' original orientation, you can leave about an inch of the band to serve as reinforcement for the new one.

Step 3: Cut the cups apart. Some dancers avoid doing this and will leave the cups together. If you want to reorient the cups, tilt them up, or bring them closer together, you will want to remove this center panel or strip.

Bra Cups

While there are many bras that have decorative covers, such as velvet or brocade, most bras come in the standard white, ivory, black, and red. Push-up varieties tend to be a bit more festive than strapless styles, but most of these fabrics cannot be matched, so making a coordinating hip belt may out of the question. However, a plain black velvet bra might serve very well as-is. Another option is to use a nice bra to coordinate with a shimmy belt of the same color. But if you want complete coordination, plan on covering your cups to get a perfect match between your bra and belt.

Stabilizing the Cups

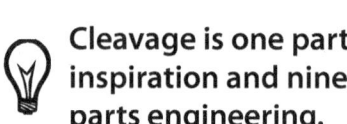 **Cleavage is one part inspiration and nine parts engineering.**

While many bras will be perfectly shaped and firm enough to support a complex surface embellishment with beaded fringe or heavy coins, some may not. Not all firm-cupped or padded bras are built identically, so additional stabilization may be needed to help create the optimal stiffness. How can you tell if your bra will support a lot of trim? Pin some decorations on and see what happens. If the cup collapses when you lay it on a table, it's not going to be able to support both you and the decoration. When you put the bra on and give it a shake, does the fabric give, allowing your bust to move? If it doesn't keep your bustline in place, then you will need to reinforce the fabric to control any excessive movement.

All-over reinforcement involves using a stabilizing fabric to completely cover the cups. There are three types of materials that can be used to really firm up the bra cups.

Buckram. This heavy woven fabric is often stiffened with starch to give it stability. It comes in several different weights and is used extensively in the hat making industry. Most fabric stores that have a bridal department will sell buckram.

Hair canvas. Horsehair, camelhair, or Hymo are all synonyms for hair canvas. This gray fabric is very sturdy and strong and is used extensively in formal tailoring to control and shape suits and lapels. It's surprisingly thin and will not add much thickness to the bra cups.

Interfacing. Interfacing comes in a wide variety of styles and weights, in fusible and non-fusible varieties. For bra reinforcement, a non-fusible variety works well and saves a few pennies. Look for heavyweight interfacing in either woven or non-woven styles.

Reshaping the Cups

The shape of the cup is not set in stone. You can cut into the material or build out from the material to change the shape of the upper edge. This change in shape can be either a structural change or it can be an extension of the applied surface design. If you decide that it's a just a surface design issue, then you can proceed to the next step of making the pattern for the bra cup cover.

Just remember, if you cut into your cups you will need to reinforce the clipped edge. Use a strip of grosgrain ribbon on the inside of the cup to add stability. To cover the cut edge, use double fold bias tape to secure it.

If you plan on using wire on the edges of your bra cups, you can overcast the wire onto the edge of the cup and then cover it with the binding.

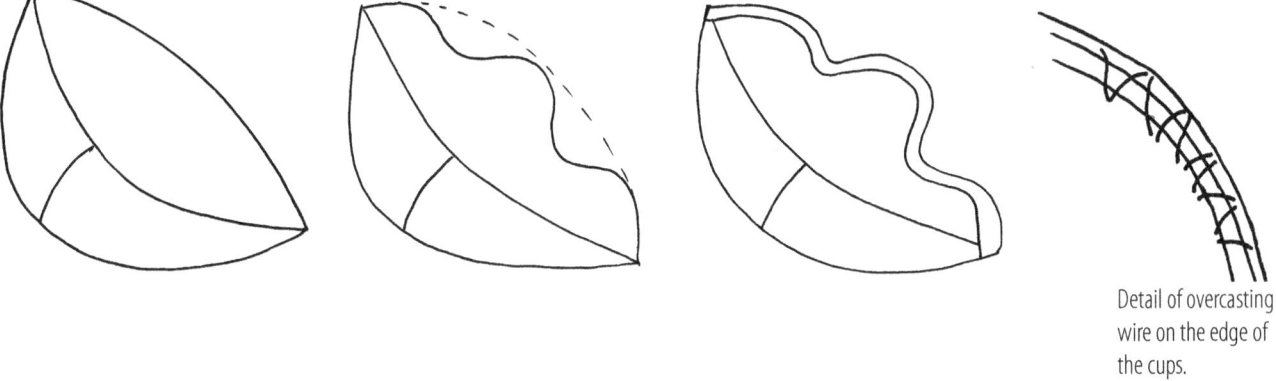

Detail of overcasting wire on the edge of the cups.

Making the Pattern

If you are using inexpensive fabric, and don't mind wasting a bit, you can skip making a pattern. However, if you are using beaded, sequined, or very expensive fabrics, you will want to conserve as much of the cloth as you can. To make this possible, you must make a pattern of your bra cups. Cut your final covering cloth out, and then stitch it down {{to what??}}. Simply follow the directions below for covering the cups and drape them with an inexpensive fabric, such as muslin or gingham. When you have arrived at step 6, draw a line around the outside of the cup. Make sure to mark the darts as well. When you remove it from the bra, you will have a custom-fitted cover for that bra. Add an inch (25 mm) of seam allowance around your pattern.

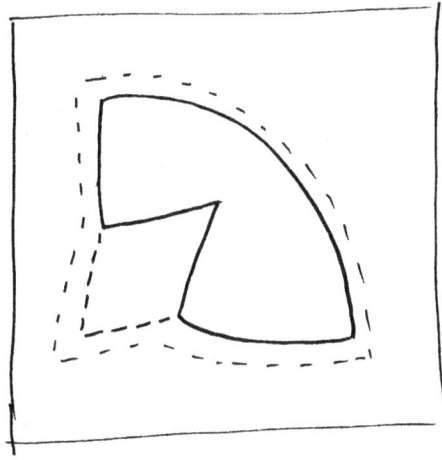

Covering the Cups

Step 1: Cut two pieces of covering fabric approximately 2-3 inches (5–8 cm) larger than the cups. When in doubt, go bigger. You can always trim excess fabric.

Step 2: Beginning at one corner, gently fold the fabric over the top of the cup, pinning as you work your way across. When you get to the corner, trim away excess fabric and fold the corner under.

Step 3: Continue folding and pinning, working your way across the lower edge of the cup. Pause when you get to the center of the cup.

Step 4: Begin pinning at opposite corner, making sure to trim and eliminate excess fabric. Work your way along the bottom edge towards the center where you stopped before.

Step 5: You will find you have a large pleat of fabric. This will form your dart. Smooth the dart towards the outside corner. The dart can go either way, but towards the outside is the most common style.

Step 6: Pin down the dart area.

Step 7: Flip the cup over. Trim excess fabric. Whip stitch the covering of the bra to the inside. When you are done, flip the bra over and slip stitch the dart down.

Now the cup is ready to be decorated and stitched back into the shape of the bra. Some designers like to leave the two cups attached at the middle. If you choose to do this, cover the center panel of the bra with fabric first, then cover the bra cups. when you get to this center panel, instead of folding the corners under you will fold the fabric under and slip stitch along the fold.

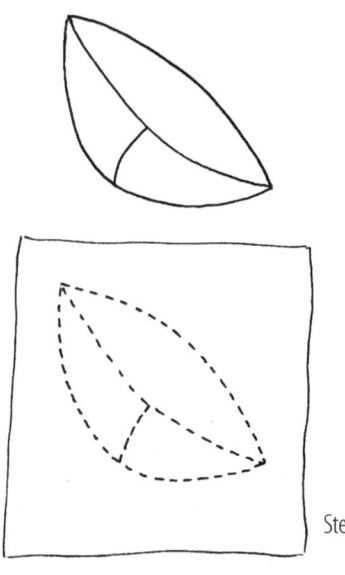
Step 1

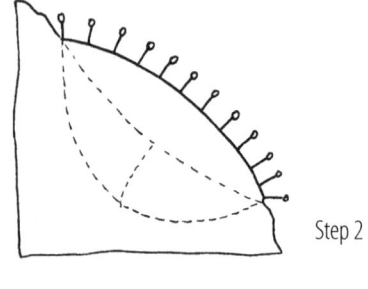
Step 2

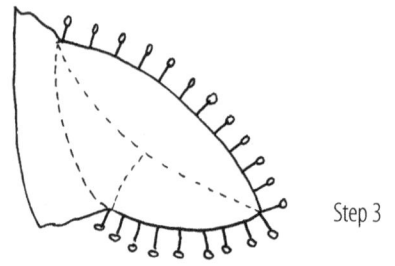
Step 3

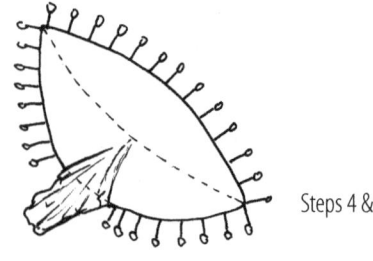
Steps 4 & 5

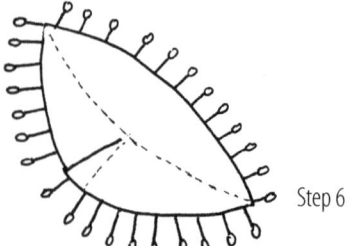
Step 6

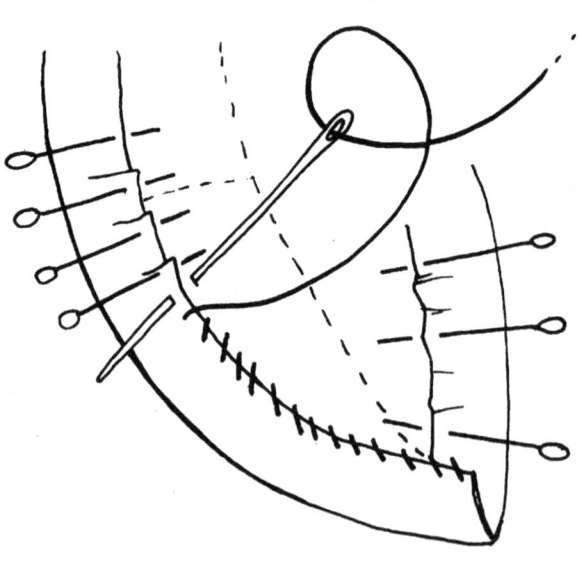
Step 7: Stitching down the fabric

Fringe Placement

The bra offers a fairly limited space for surface embellishments. The cup is also dimensional, being curved and rounded. So fringe moves optimally when hung at or below the bust point. Here are a few layouts for applying fringe for maximum movement.

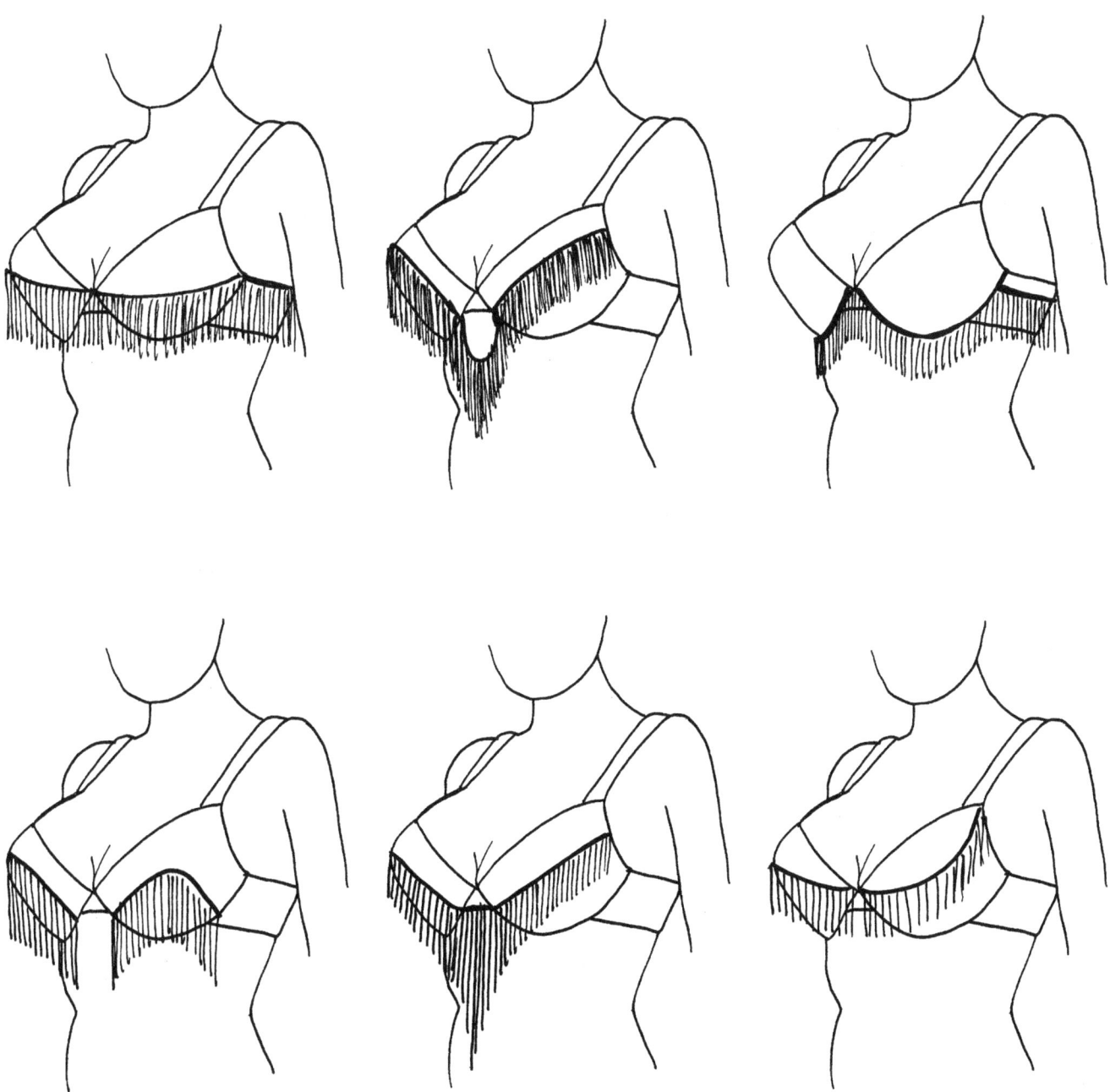

Reconstruction

Once the cups have been decorated, the next step in the process is to reconstruct the bra.

Center Front

Reconnecting the center front can be accomplished in several ways. At its most basic, a simple tab of sturdy ribbon can be used to hold the cups together. If you are looking for a more shaped look, use a central panel made from two layers of reinforced interfacing covered with the same fabric as the cups. After shaping your center front piece, stitch it onto the cup on the inside using a strong secure whip stitch. On the outside of the bra, slip stitch the cup to the center panel using invisible stitching.

Some dancers like to construct their bras with a closure in the center front. If this is your style, make sure that the closure is solid and sturdy because if this comes loose during a performance, you might find yourself more exposed than you would like. For security's sake, resist using plastic bra hooks. Sturdy metal hooks, or even secure belt buckle, will form a secure front closure.

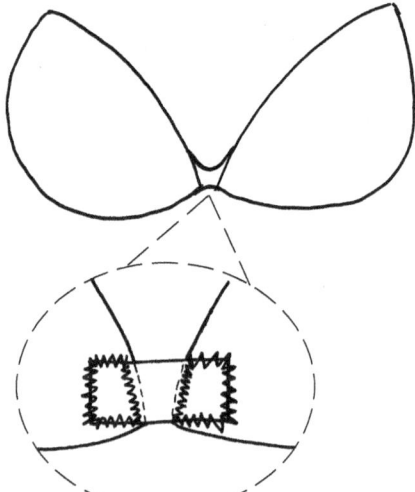

Center front tab detail seen from the inside. Zig-zag hand stiching.

Chest Band

From a structural point of view, the chest band is actually the most important feature of the bra. If the chest band isn't sturdy enough, the bra will shift and move around the body as the dancer performs. The band is generally a single strap that runs from one side of the bra to another. A V-shaped piece of grosgrain ribbon attached at the sides of the bra will help maintain stability. There is no magical formula for figuring out what the best placement of these stabilizing bands. At this point in the costume construction, it's a matter of pinning, adjusting, and pinning again.

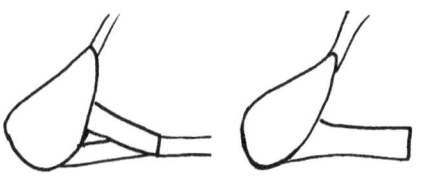

Left: Chest band.
Right: Shaped chest band made from interfacing.

Straps

After the cups have been re-attached at the center, and the chest band stitched on, the next step is the straps. Grosgrain ribbon is strong, stable, and comes in a variety of colors and widths. I like to use two or even three layers stitched together for my straps. Once your cups are done, the only really good way to get a good fit is to pin the straps into place and try the bra on. Pin and play is the only way!

 Side support is important. Make sure that your bra has straps wide enough to support the entire cup.

There are several different strap styles. The variations that draw closer to the neck such as the "V" and the collar will create the illusion of a more ample bustline and create more cleavage.

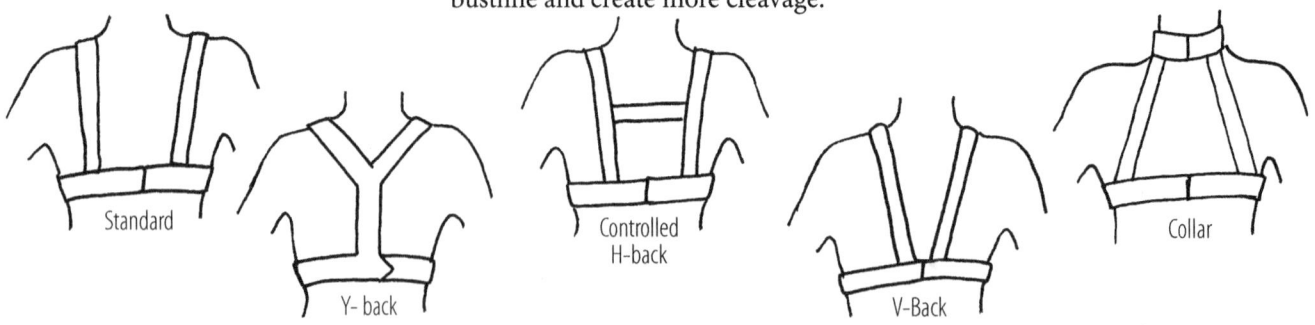

Finishing Touches

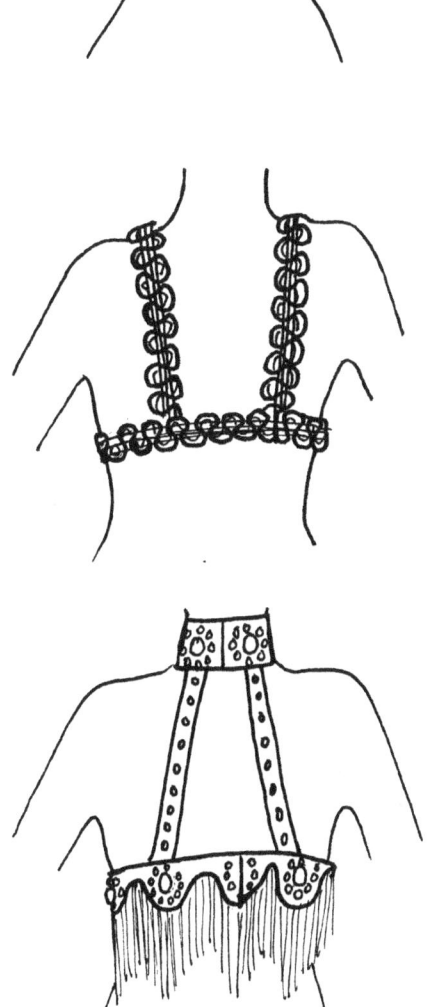

With the cups together and the straps stitched on, the final step in bra production is the decoration of the straps. While straps are the structural element that keeps the garment firmly attached to the body, they need to be worked into the design program of the piece. It's important for a designer to consider that the costume is a work of art that is viewed in the round. The audience will see the front, back, and sides as the dancer moves and performs.

Decorating the Straps

Before you contemplate decorating the straps, make sure your bra fits the way you want it to. Put some music on and dance in your bra. Really test the straps with shoulder shimmies, arm movements, and torso twisting. Make any adjustments that are necessary at this time. Once you start decorating, it will become more difficult to make changes in the fit. It won't be impossible, but definitely more work.

If you use a grosgrain ribbon in a color that harmonizes with or matches your costume, you can simply run a row of braid over your straps. If the material is not really visually exciting, you can stitch a tube of the bra covering fabric around the strap. Once you have the strap covered, you can go on to use a variety of surface design techniques to embellish. Straps can be beaded, embellished with ribbons, sequins on string, or have small appliqués in key focal points.

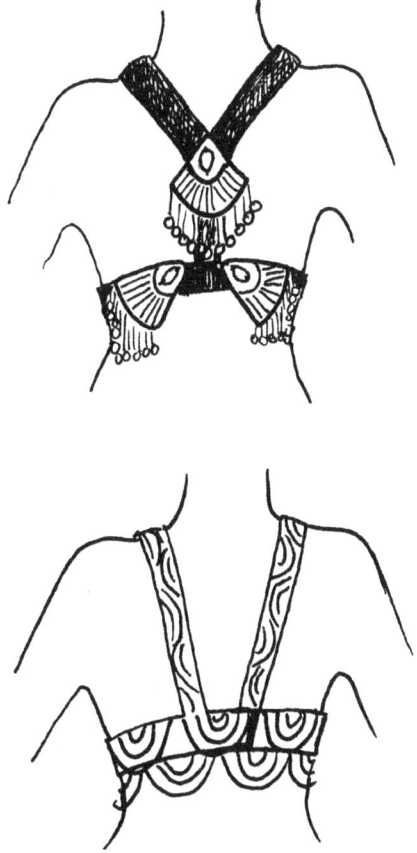

Large Size Options

Many large-sized dancers lament the lack of firm-cupped, padded, or push-up bras available in their sizes. While specialty lingerie stores carry suitable styles that can sometimes go up to a 42DD, this still leaves some women wondering what to do. An ample bust line should not be an obstacle to designing a lovely costume or performing. Here are a few ideas for conquering this challenge:

- **Wear a vest.** Instead of making a beaded bra, why not make a fitted, shaped vest and bead, embroidery and embellish it the same way you would a bra. A vest can be very fitted, cutting low to expose your ample cleavage and reinforced to allow the use of dramatic, yet heavy, beaded fringe.

- **Build a bra from scratch.** Although this option is beyond the scope of this book, it is one path that some dancers choose. There are patterns and specialty supplies available mail order, from fiberfill for the cups, power net for the chest band, to the all-important underwires. For suppliers, consult the resources list at the back of the book.

- **Stiffen a bra.** One kind of messy but fun project is to transform a soft cup bra. This technique involves using a fabric stiffener on the bra. How do you get the shape? It's easy to describe. Wrap your upper torso loosely in kitchen plastic wrap. This is to keep the glue from adhering to your body. Put your bra on over the plastic, adjusting it until you get the perfect fit. Next, apply fabric stiffener and allow to dry. When you remove your bra, you will have some shaped firm cups that just need to have padding added to the inside and be covered with decorative fabric.

Fitted vest.

Peasant blouse with vest will cover a standard bra.

8 Belt Construction

The belt is one of the key features of the dancer's costume. The vocabulary of Middle Eastern dance movement is centered on subtle motions of the hips. From shimmies and drops to figure eight's and bumps, the belt is designed to draw the viewer's eye right to the center of these motions. Dangling surface design elements such as fringe, paillettes, coins, and beads will amplify the motion, allowing viewers further back in the audience to see even the most subtle of moves.

Unlike the finished costume bra, which can be developed from a purchased lingerie base, the belt gets built up from scratch. The belt must coordinate with the bra, fit very well, and support the surface decoration.

Fit is exceptionally important when it comes to the belt. If it's too tight it will creep up the hips. If it's too loose, and it might twist around the body as you shimmy and shake. An incorrectly shaped belt, with the incorrectly-sized or misplaced darts, might slide upwards or downwards. If no darts or shaping is present, you might find the belt gapping at the center in the back.

Belt Features

As one of the most essential costume pieces, the belt can be as simple as a straight line around the hips, or as complex as an intricate strappy design with wired appliques that extend beyond the edges of the belt. At its core foundation, there are only three fundamental styles of belt structure.

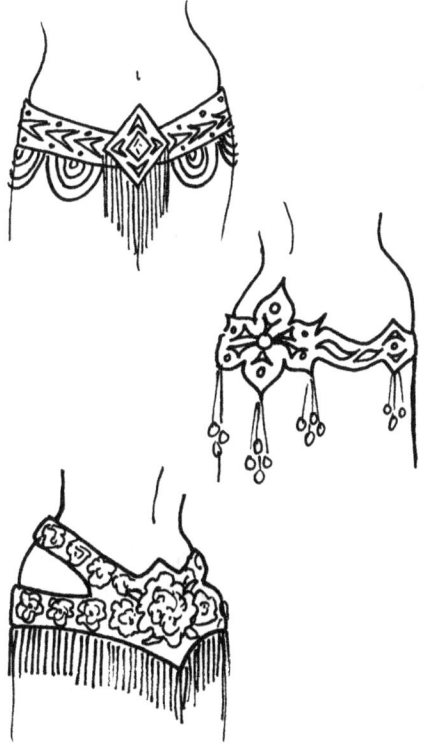

Central closure. This style of belt is a boon to the novice designer because it instantly creates a focal point. This closure could be a geometric shape, an abstract design, or an iconic image. However, this style of belt is more difficult to adjust unless the closure is placed asymmetrically.

Two-piece with side closure. This style of belt is the easiest to fit and adjust. If you experience major shifts in weight, or plan on selling your costume in the future, this is the most easily alterable design.

Strap extensions. Straps that extend up to connect to the bra, reach up and around the waist, or over and across the hip have been quite popular in the last five years. This style of belt requires a more precise fitting.

Integrated belt. Some dancers prefer to attach their belt to their skirt, or to treat the top or waist of their skirt like a belt. If you are making a straight skirt with fabric that stretches, you will need to support the top of the skirt with an interlining in order to support heavy beading. There are lots of options for this style of costume. It is currently very popular with designers overseas.

Making the Pattern

The best way to achieve an optimal fit is to have a belt custom draped on your body. Unfortunately, it's virtually impossible to effectively drape yourself. This project requires an extra set of hands, and it can be fun for a group. Wear a close-fitting garment such as a leotard, unitard, leggings, or even your underwear.

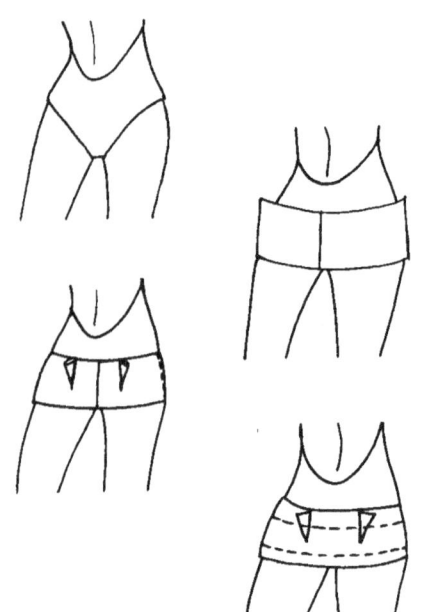

Step 1: Cut two strips of cloth approximately 12" (30 cm) deep and long enough to go around your hips.

Step 2: Beginning on the back, pin the center of one piece of cloth to the center of your back at approximately the level of the belt. Smooth the fabric outward along the top about 3" (75 mm) from the center and pin.

Step 3: Smooth the cloth out around the fullest part of the body and pin at the side. Make sure not to stretch the cloth.

Step 4: Working from the side, smooth the top edge towards the center. When you reach the pin, you will discover that you have formed a pleat approximately 3" (75 mm) from the center. This will form the top of your dart.

Step 5: Repeat the above steps with the front side.

Step 6: Pin the darts down and using a pencil mark their legs.

Step 7: Now's the time to actually design! Sketch the shape of your belt onto the cloth.

Step 8: Look in a mirror to give yourself a sense of distance. Do you like the shape of the belt? Make any design modifications and adjustments while it's still pinned to the body.

Step 9: If you plan on having straps that reach over the hip, now is the time to experiment with placement using grosgrain ribbon. Start at the front of the belt and pin the ribbons into position. Pull the ribbon over the hips and lay in the desired position. Pin at the back and mark not only the placement on the belt, but the angle on the ribbon as well.

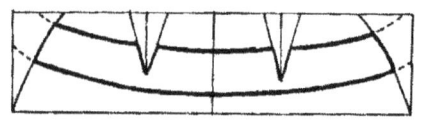

Step 10: Mark your pattern. Pay special attention to these points:

- Center Front
- Center Back
- Side seams
- Strap locations (if needed)
- Dart positions

Step 11: Remove the pattern from the body and go over the lines with a fine felt-tipped marker. Add length at the opening. Generally the back is the "under" side and should be about 2" (5 cm) longer than the front. The front should end at the side seam, although some dancers add an inch to allow for future expansion.

Step 12: Make a test sample of your belt out of a stiff-non-stretching fabric. Test the fit and make any necessary adjustments in the style lines.

Dart Elimination

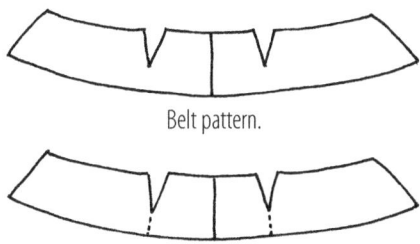
Belt pattern.

Draw lines up from the lower edge. Cut along these lines up to (but not through) the darts.

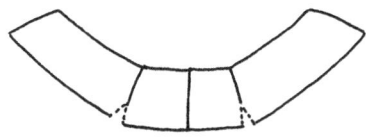
Swing the dart legs closed and tape shut.

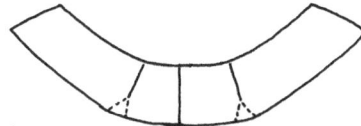
Smooth out the bottom and top edges.

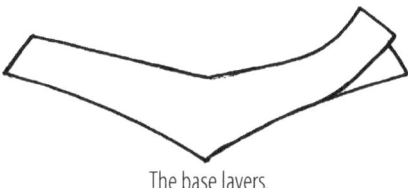
The base layers.

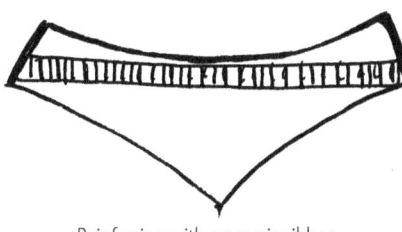
Reinforcing with grosgrain ribbon.

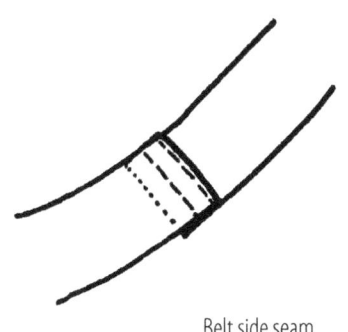
Belt side seam.

Step 13: Take your sample apart and use it to make a paper pattern. Be sure to transfer all key marks and date it. If the bottom edge of your dart disappears, merely tape the separated edges of the pattern together. This will eliminate the dart, but preserve the shape of the garment.

If you have a full dart on your pattern, it will save you many headaches if you eliminate your dart by moving it to the bottom edge. Draw a line from the bottom edge of the belt to the end of the dart. See the illustrations at left to complete this step.

The Belt Base

Once you have a pattern that fits your body you are ready to build the belt. A good solid sturdy base will provide your belt with stability and strength and is worth the extra time and expense. There are many different combinations of materials and techniques for making a belt. Always consult fellow dancers, teachers, and costumers for their favorite tips on stitching the perfect base. Then mix and match their hints and tips together to develop your own method for belt construction.

Building the Base

Use the pattern you draped on your body to create the belt base. The belt base needs to be sturdy and structurally sound, so make sure that your layers are firmly adhered so that the weight of your embellishments does not cause the belt to sag or buckle. The base should be made without seam allowances. Here is one approach for building a base.

The base layer. The stiffest material you can locate should be used as the first layer of your belt. Buckram, hair canvas, or even plastic needlepoint canvas can make a good, solid first layer. I prefer to use buckram because it is both thin and strong. Needlepoint canvas adds a lot of bulk, and though some dancers use it to great effect, it is difficult to stitch through and you cannot use a sewing machine!

Reinforce. On both sides of this first layer, reinforce with a heavyweight fusible interfacing. This will keep the belt from pulling or stretching on the bias and will add rigidity to the foundation.

Add padding. The next layer gets applied to the outer side of the belt. Flannel, polar fleece, craft felt, or lightweight poly-fill are just a few of the materials that will work to bulk out the belt. A layer of fusible webbing will bind these layers without adding stitching.

Reinforce at the level of most stress. Using grosgrain ribbon, or petersham, stitch or fuse a ribbon around the belt at the same level where you will be placing your closure. If your belt has a straight upper edge, this can go here. If your belt has a shaped edge, place the ribbon at the level where it can wrap entirely around your body.

When you have all these layers in place, your belt is ready to be covered. Some dancers like to add a layer of plastic, rubber or latex as a barrier for perspiration. In my experience, I prefer to use liquid latex after the surface

embellishments have been applied, but before the final lining is installed. Applying it after all the stitching is in place acts as a reinforcing glue, further protecting the stitches and locking the knots into position.

Purchasing a Ready-Made Belt Base

There are vendors who carry pre-assembled belt bases that eliminate the pattern making and base construction steps. When you purchase a base, make sure that you get what you need. Look for these features:

Shape. The belt base should be a pleasing shape. Many pre-made belt bases come in standard shapes such as a sweetheart, scoop or angled designed. Belt bases that are composed of two parts, a front and a back, will offer you the easiest fit adjustments.

Size. The base should be long enough to reach completely around you. A two piece belt should have a one inch overlap on both sides. A one piece belt, with a central medallion should overlap about an inch and a half.

Coverage. Make sure that the belt offers you enough coverage, so that the side is wide enough, the central shaped areas are deep enough to fit your planned surface design, and to provide a good proportion for your figure.

Materials. The belt base needs to be stiff and sturdy enough to support beaded fringe or heavy coins. Look for a multi-layer construction that is quite stiff. You should not be able to fold the belting base without it creasing or cracking. Look for combinations of buckram, heavy-duty interfacing and a padding layer of polyfiber or felt.

Before you cover your belt base, add a row of grosgrain ribbon to reinforce the belt and prevent it from stretching. You may want to add an additional layer of padding to bulk out your belt.

Fitting the Belt

If you have made a custom belt, your base should fit pretty well. If, however, you purchased a pre-made belt, you might have to experiment and work on the fit. Pin the belt base together and place it around your hips to test the fit. You may have to do some trimming to make the belt fit perfectly around your hips. If you find your belt comes together at an angle, you can trim it even or try adjusting the angle to fit better.

Trim and adjust your belt base before covering. No matter if you are making it yourself or using a pre-made base, you will want to adjust your belt for optimum fit.

Covering the Belt

Once you have your base made, the next major step is to cover your belt. While you might be tempted to stitch your belt covering on using a sewing machine, this can lead to problems because the machine stitching pulls the fabric tight across the base. While this may look wonderful when the belt base is flat, when it comes time to wrap the base around your curved body, the fabric can stretch, pull or buckle. It's worth the extra time it takes to stitch the fabric down by hand. Hand sewing allows you to control the tension of the thread so that you can build in enough give into the belt covering.

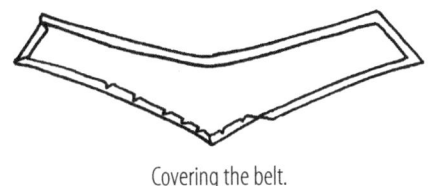
Covering the belt.

Step 1: Take your belt pattern and add an additional seam allowance. I like to use an inch seam allowance on my belts because it gives me a wide edge around the inside of the belt to attach a lining.

Step 2: Position the belt base on the covering fabric, centering it. Ensure that any surface design, such as stripes, are perfectly aligned before beginning the stitching process.

Step 3: Carefully begin folding the covering fabric over the belt base. Clip and notch the fabric to allow it to lay smoothly through the curves. As you fold it over, pin into place.

Step 4: Work your way completely around the belt. Start at the center and work your way to the outside on both the top edge and bottom. Be careful not to pull the cloth too tightly.

Belt lining.

Step 5: Before stitching, test to make sure that the belt will lay smoothly around the hips. To test, carefully position the belt around your hips to make sure it lays smoothly without puckers, pulls or bulges. Now is the time to adjust any buckling. Simply unpin, smooth and re-pin.

Step 6: Stitch the cover to the base, working from the center towards the sides. A herringbone stitch will hold the fabric securely, while allowing for give under stress. A straight stitch or running stitch might break under stress.

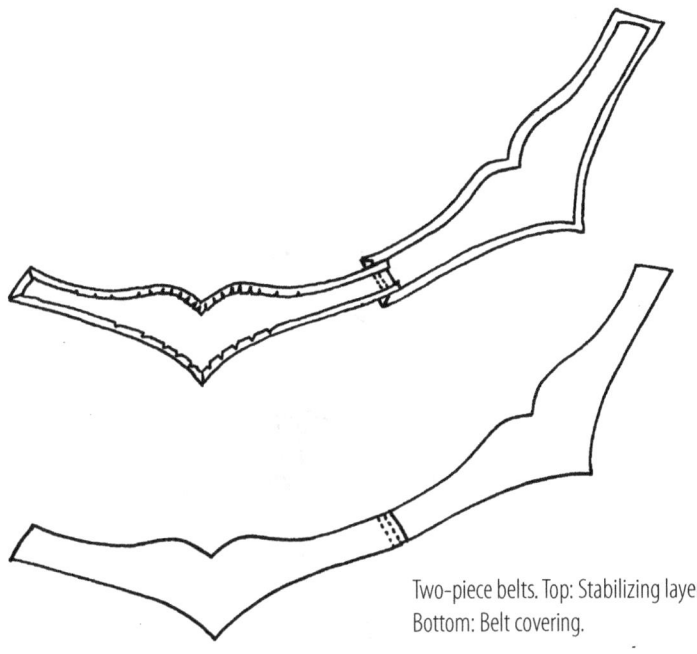

Stitch two-piece belts together on one side after covering.

Cover first to allow adjustments for weight shifts or in case of a future sale.

Two-piece belts. Top: Stabilizing layers. Bottom: Belt covering.

Embellishing the Belt

Once the belt is covered, the next step is applying the surface design details. Beads can be applied directly onto the surface, stitched into appliqués, or both. The following chapters address the process of creating beautiful beaded designs to decorate your finished belt. But to help you get started thinking of all those possible belt designs, here's a group of illustrations to inspire and get those creative juices flowing. When selecting a style consider your needs. Taller and larger women require a belt shape with more substantial coverage. By the same token, thicker belts and strong horizontal lines might overwhelm petite or slender dancers.

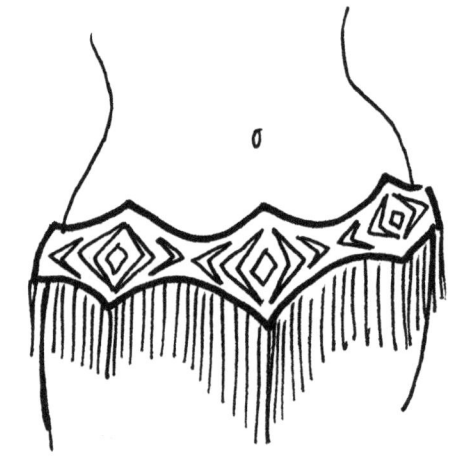

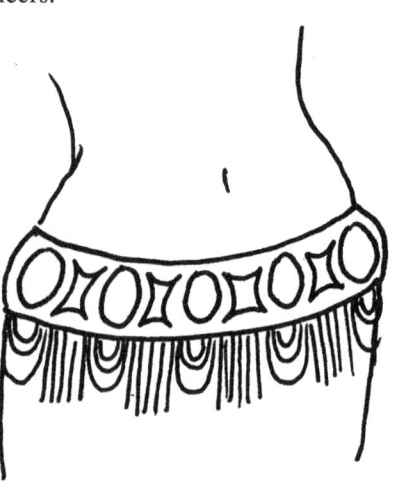

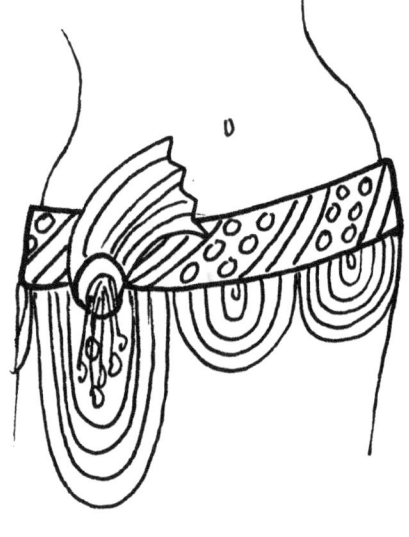

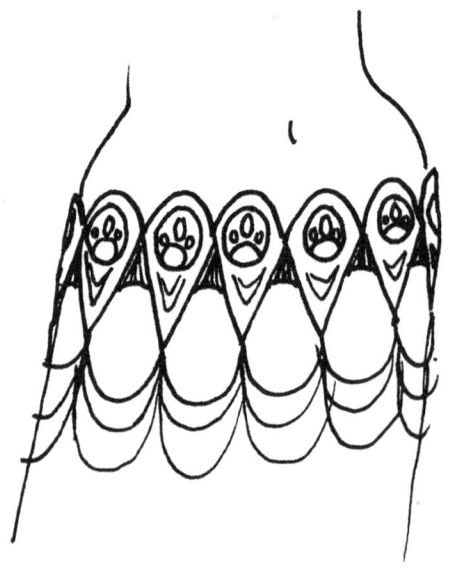

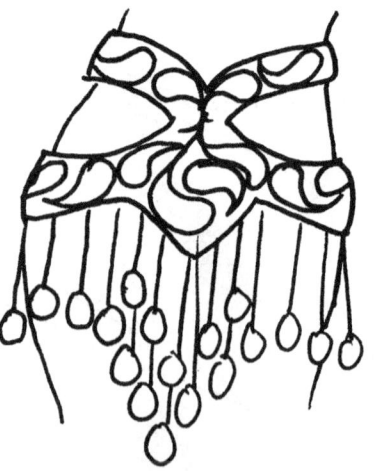

9 Surface Embellishments

Beads

Beading is a time-intensive project that requires good eyes and steady hands. Using the proper tools and having the right supplies available can ease the beading process, allowing you to work as efficiently as possible. This chapter will introduce the major groups of applied surface design elements and the essential supplies needed to complete beading projects, such as needles and thread. Methods and techniques for application are discussed in the following chapters.

There are many styles of beads available for bead embroidery; too many to discuss in a few pages. For more complete discussions of beads, consult one of the many informative beading books currently available. Some of the most useful titles are listed in the beads and beading section of the bibliography.

While most beading books are geared towards jewelry makers, keep your eyes opened for publications with chapters on surface beading, bead embroidery, or fabric beadwork. Also look for useful books in the embroidery and surface embellishment sections of the bookstore.

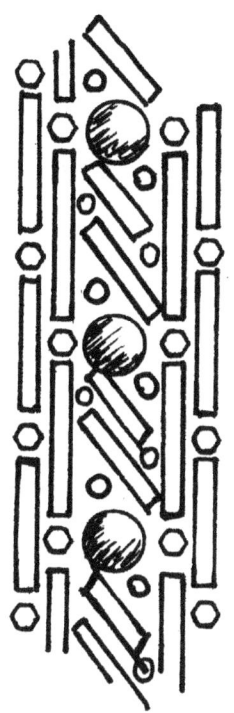

Bugles and seeds are the two bead styles most commonly used for surface embellishments on Middle Eastern dancewear. However, when you go into your favorite bead shop don't limit yourself to these two styles of beads. Look around and explore the variety and options available to you. There is a myriad of interesting glass, plastic, metal, and stone beads that can be integrated into the surface design of your costumes. Larger beads make for quicker beading, especially when making fringe. Smaller beads will create a more uniform surface when applied as a surface design.

About Beads

Beads come in a wide a variety of shapes. The most common shapes used in beaded embroidery are round, faceted, barrel, and drop. Flat beads and irregular stone chips can be similarly applied to sequins to add texture. There are almost as many materials as there are bead shapes. While many dancers prefer glass, crystal, or plastic beads, some alternatives can add a distinctive touch to your costumes, including metal, wood, semi-precious stones, ceramic, shells, and more. The key is to shop around and explore with your designer's eye roving and your mind open to new ideas. When selecting beads, keep a couple of things in mind:

Faceted, drop, barrel, and spherical bead shapes.

- **Beads should be smooth.** Rough, sharp or jagged edges can catch and snag on skirts, veils and arm decorations. Rough beads are more prone to break their threads, shortening the life span of the garment.

- **Size is important.** The larger the bead, the more weight it will add to your costume. Consider how heavy the supporting layers are before applying very large beads. In general, most dancers like to use beads 7 mm or smaller for surface applications.
- **Consider the durability.** Some media will break down faster than others. Very long bugles can fracture and break, slicing through the supporting threads. Unfired ceramic beads will break down and could crumble under pressure.

Bugle Beads

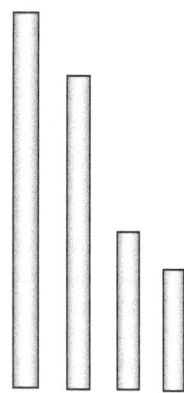

Bugle beads are long tubular glass beads. They are available in a wide variety of colors and are frequently manufactured with matching rocailles. They can be found in shops sized by number, 1 (the shortest) to 5. However, many vendors sell bugles based on their length in millimeters. The diameter of bugle beads is similar to an 11 or 12 seed bead. Bugles come in smooth or twisted varieties and in a wide range of colors that vary with the season.

Bugles are excellent beads for filling in large spaces of colors and can be used to build complex patterns. Because they are made of glass, the longer lengths can be fragile. The edges of bugles can be sharp, which may cut through or abrade the supporting thread. You will need beading needles to apply longer bugles to the surface of the fabric. Beading needles are longer and thinner than standard sewing needles and can pass through the longer beads with ease. Because of their linear quality, bugles are an excellent choice for use in geometric patterns making repeated designs easy to develop.

Seed Beads

Seed beads are sized by number: the higher the number, the smaller the bead. There are many different varieties of seed beads, most are available between the sizes of 7 to 14, with variations in shape. Color availability will vary with your suppliers and follow the current fashion trends.

Czech seed beads. These small glass beads tend to be flatter and somewhat irregular in shape. They are available in a variety of finishes. The holes can be quite fine and in any bag or string of them you may find that there are seeds that have holes too small for use.

Japanese seed beads. Available in sizes 11 and 14, the Japanese style seed beads are thicker, rounded, and tend to have larger holes making them easier to string. They tend to be more uniform in size than Czech beads.

Delica. Another type of Japanese glass bead, the Delica is cut from a cane and is not rounded off, giving them a cylindrical shape. The holes on these are very large, making them an ideal choice for embroidery. Because these are regular in size and shape, they are a favorite of bead weavers and are easily found in most bead specialty stores. They come in two sizes. There is a regular size that's similar to an 11 or 12, and there is also a larger size probably equal to about an 8 or 7.

Charlottes (Czech one-cuts). This term refers to an irregular cut glass seed bead. The holes in these can vary in size. They tend to be quite small and come in sizes 11, 13, and 14.

Surface Embellishments

Rocailles. These are silver-lined glass beads, sometimes with a lining in a contrasting color. They are widely available in many colors. Most Egyptian beaded fringe is made from rocaille beads. They are available in many sizes, although the easiest to find seems to be an 11 or 12.

Other Decorative Elements

Along with beads, there are many other elements that can be integrated into your beadwork. Pearls, rhinestones, sequins, and paillettes are just a few of the most popular alternatives to beads. Here is a list of some of the most readily available items.

Sequins

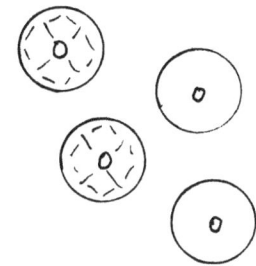

Sequins come in two major styles: flat or cup. They are available loose or stitched onto strings, into braid, or onto the surface of cloth. Sequins add a great deal of shine and are relatively inexpensive. Historically, small metal disks have been integrated into the costumes of people throughout the Middle East. An assortment of finishes are available; including holographic, multicolored, and metallic. The surface of sequins can deteriorate when exposed to perspiration, becoming clear or silvery. Spray coating them with acrylic can extend the life of the sequins.

Spangles

A variant on the sequin is the spangle. Larger than sequins, spangles are available in many standard motifs. Leaves, hearts, and stars are just a few of the easiest to locate styles. Spangles are generally flat although they occasionally have a pattern carved into the surface, such as veins on leaves, to give them a multi-dimensional look. The hole can be located at the center or at one end.

Paillettes

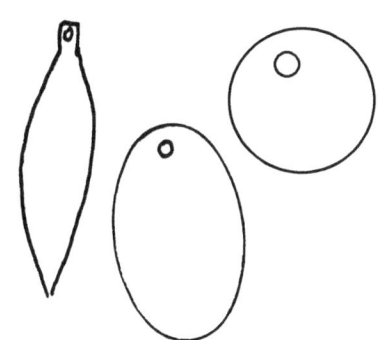

Paillettes are basically very large, flat sequins. They have holes at the top and come in a variety of size and shapes. Circles come in 1/2", 3/4", and 1" sizes and in an assortment of colors. Ovals and teardrops are also available. Holographic paillettes sparkle and really catch the eye when they move. Paillettes are a bit harder to find than sequins; consult your favorite dance vendor if you cannot find any at your local bead or trim shop. Many dancers like to use paillettes as accents at the tips of fringe, or in rows along the bottom edges of costume pieces. A waisted loop attachment will allow the paillette to flip and move easily.

Rhinestones

Are available in three major shapes: faceted, flat back, or double points. Faceted beads are cut with a hole through them can be used to make fringe with a lot of sparkle. Flat-backed rhinestones come ready to glue on or have heat-activated adhesive already applied. Rhinestones cut with double points are designed for placement into jewelry settings. They can be difficult to attach and may protrude out from the costume, catching and snagging on costume pieces, accessories, and veils. Rhinestones come in a wide variety of colors with sizes ranging from 2 mm to 7 mm or larger. The flat back styles are most ideal for costume work and come in assorted shapes including round, oval, squares, and teardrops.

Plastic Gems

Sometimes called plastic rhinestones, these faux jewels are less sparkly than their glass or crystal relatives. Available in two forms, stitch-on or glue-on, these flat-backed stones are easy to apply. They are available in a wide variety of colors, shapes and styles. From 4 mm dots to 3" (75 cm) rectangles, these gems are an inexpensive way to add sparkle, color and textures to a costume. However, be aware that craft stores can be the most expensive source for plastic gems. Look for specialty vendors in sewing and beading magazines or on the Internet.

Pearls

One of the most beautiful and elegant design elements a dancer can incorporate into her costume is the pearl. They come in several major shapes: round, teardrop, barrel, and seed. Freshwater pearls are irregular in size and shape and can add a great deal of texture to the design of a costume. Sizes vary from 0.5 mm to 9 mm and the pearls can be tinted shades of pastel pink, lavender, or blue. Simulated pearls can be painted or dyed to change their color to more closely match a design.

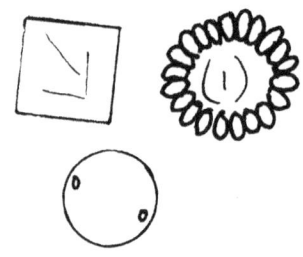

Mirrors

Although used extensively in tribal costume ensembles, mirrors can make a good addition to more upscale beaded ensembles as well. Mirrors come in round and square shapes. While the majority of styles require the use of adhesives or sandwiching between layers of cloth, there are varieties available that have holes that can be stitched through. Mirrors, when used in abundance, can create an unfortunate "disco ball" effect, especially when they completely cover a bra.

Coins

There are really only two major styles of coins: authentic coins that have been drilled for use as a costuming embellishment or commercially available pressed coins. Real coins can be expensive to purchase and need to be cleaned, punched or drilled, and then filed down so the holes are smooth. Real coins are heavy and make a low jingle when the dancer moves. Stamped or pressed coins are lighter and make a higher tinkling sound. They can appear brassy, overly gold, or silver, so some dancers give them a coat of paint to help reduce the shine. Coins can be applied using jump rings or a waisted loop stitch that allows the coins to flip and turn freely to maximize the sound. Spray inexpensive coins with acrylic paint before construction to preserve the finish.

Shells

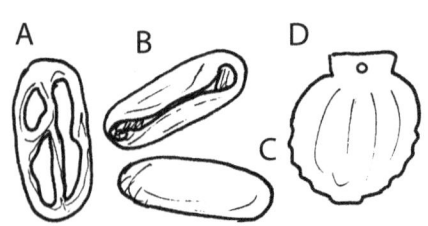

A: Sliced cowrie. B: Cowrie. C: Back side of cowrie. D: Small bivalve shell with hole.

Shells can be an ideal surface embellishment for tribal-esque or folkloric styles of costumes. Specialty costumes with African or Caribbean themes can

Surface Embellishments

look magnificent with shell accents. Cowry shells are the most commonly available and can be purchased from many bead vendors. They can be either stitched on (if they have been drilled) or glued on. Other types of shells can be used in costuming as well; look for ease of application and size.

Pre-Made Fringe

Many dancers find fringe construction to be tedious. But fear not, for there are many styles of fringe commercially available. From soft rayon fringe to elaborately beaded styles, options abound from specialty vendors and at fabric or craft stores. These fringe types usually have an unattractive tape or strip at the top of the fringe, so be prepared to work in masking elements to hide the supporting strip.

Chainette Fringe

Made from rayon, chainette fringe is available from fabric shops, craft centers, and upholstery stores. Available in white, black, red, and gold, along with assorted colors that vary with the seasons, this fringe is versatile, hand washable, and easy to work with. There are also variations with tassels. Some chainette fringe comes with a decorative band of braid at the top, while others have a rather undecorative stitched edge. White chainette fringe is dyable with custom colors that can be used to make totally unique one-of-a-kind embellishments. This fringe can also be rolled and stitched to make tassels.

Commercial Beaded Fringe

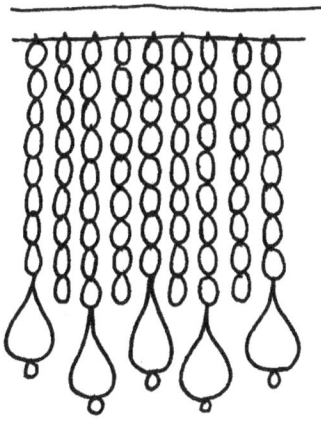

Some fabric stores, especially shops that specialize in evening or bridal wear, will have a selection of commercially beaded fringe. In general, commercially beaded fringe tends to be more widely spaced, uses bigger or longer beads, and comes in a limited range of colors. Black and white are the easiest to find although red, gold, and silver are other frequently stocked colors. Commercially beaded fringe is usually mounted on twill tape, which makes this an easy product to stitch on with a sewing machine. But the tape is unattractive and when planning to use these products you should try to hide it. The most common shapes and styles of fringe are individual strands and loops. One off-beat source for commercial fringe is suppliers who specialize in beaded fringe for Victorian lamps.

Egyptian Fringe

This fringe is very distinctive, thick, and lush. It is created with seed beads mounted on strands that hang in several lengths. The most common lengths are 4", 8", and 12", although longer lengths up to 18" are not uncommon. The standard measure of this style of fringe is one meter. Along with basic colors, each season brings new colors. Variegated and striped varieties can sometime be found, although they are less common than solid colors. Some vendors sell sets composed of shaped pieces, hip belt front, back, bra cover, and a short length for using as strap decoration. Occasionally, the fringe will be fabricated with decorative paillettes or metallic beads worked into a design. Egyptian fringe is available from specialty belly dance vendors; ask your favorite vendor about the color and selection they have in stock. Check the resources list at the back of this book.

Jewelry as Fringe

It is possible to utilize jewelry to provide movement and action to your costume. Earrings stitched on and allowed to hang can replace a beaded tassel. A necklace suspended from the hem of a belt or from the cups of a bra can stand in for more time consuming or budget-busting fringe. This is a great opportunity to recycle old jewelry pieces. Select your necklaces to complement your costume. A lovely rhinestone necklace will harmonize with a costume sprinkled with beads and rhinestones. Ethnic jewelry pieces can accent a tribal, Gypsy, or folkloric style. If you are making a costume embellished with pearls, you will find that pearl necklaces can be an inexpensive way to get a luxurious cascade of swags.

Don't feel limited to using necklaces, either. Earrings are an excellent jewelry option that can be effectively used to develop a matched design for your bra. Split the pairs up and utilize one on each cup. Broaches can be used as focal points at the center of the bra where the cups come together or in the middle of a focal point design on the front or back of the belt. When shopping for jewelry, keep your eyes peeled and your creative juices flowing. If you feel inspired, buy several pairs and cluster them for effect.

Chain

Last but not least, chain fringe can be used to quickly create swags around the costume. Chain was quite popular in the 60s and 70s and makes an exciting retro look, especially when combined with coins and chainette fringe. Use jump rings to attach coins and jewelry pieces to the chain. Chain can tarnish, so spray it with an acrylic sealer before stitching onto the costume to extend the life of the decoration. Look for well-made, fairly lightweight chain at craft centers and hardware stores. Run your hands over the chain to ensure that the metal is smooth and free of burrs that can catch and snag fabric.

Surface Embellishment Supplies

The supplies you use to apply your embellishments will affect not only the durability of the costume, but also the construction time. Good tools and supplies save time and make the work go smoother. Even when using inexpensive or found objects, make the investment in good needles and thread.

Needles

Select your needle based on the needs of your specific set of materials. Here are some of the factors to consider when choosing a needle:

- **Size.** The size of the holes of the beads you have chosen will determine how fine the needle needs to be.

- **Fabric.** Knit fabrics requires a ball pointed needle to prevent piercing the threads and causing runs.

- **Technique.** If you are planning on doing lots of short stitches, a shorter needle might work fine. However, if you are doing fringe, you might prefer a longer beading needle.

Surface Embellishments

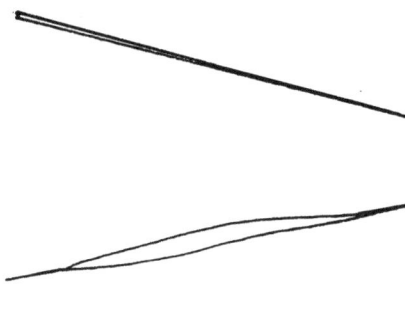

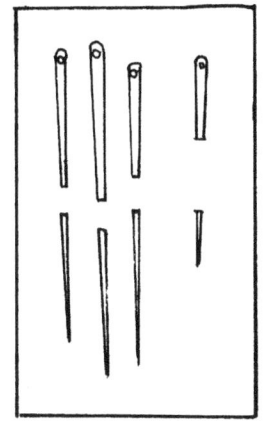

Have an assortment of needles available for different needs.

Beading needles. These are long, slender needles made from wire, so they are very flexible. They are essential for stringing fringe, making beaded netting, or making beaded tassels. Because they are so slender, the eyes can break if the thread is tugged too hard. They don't have very sharp points and might have trouble getting through some synthetic fabrics.

Big eye needles. Although not terribly sharp, these wonderful beading needles are fabulous for making fringe and for doing surface embroidery on loosely woven fabrics. The tremendous benefit of using a big eye needle is the ease of threading. These needles are made from two wires and the entire length of the needles is the eye. Even embroidery floss or crochet thread can be threaded onto these needles.

Embroidery needles. Because embroidery thread is thick, these needles have large eyes and are relatively easy to thread. However, you give up some slenderness for that big eye and they will not slip easily through the smaller seed beads.

Sharps. These are ideal for sewing beads to woven cloth. They are short and very sharp. They are available in a variety of widths; the larger the number, the smaller the needle. However, sharps can be difficult to thread due to the very small eye.

Ball point needles. The needles are designed for use with knitted fabrics. The blunt tip allows the needle to slide between the loops of the fabric preventing snags, pulls, and runs. These needles can be rather thick and may not pass easily through very small seed beads.

Thread

There are many different types of thread available at specialty bead shops, craft centers, and fabric stores. Selecting a thread can be complicated. With so many options, deciding what is best for your application can be challenging. Here are the thread types that I use most often in my beadwork.

Cotton-wrapped polyester. Available nearly everywhere and in a myriad of colors, this is the standard sewing thread and can be used to stitch most parts of the costume. When it comes to beadwork, this type of thread will work if you double it to increase its strength.

Quilting thread. This 100% cotton thread is a good choice for doing bead embroidery. It is very strong and comes in a variety of colors. However, it tends to stretch which can be a liability when making fringe.

Button and carpet threads. These are both thicker and stronger versions of the cotton-wrapped polyester thread. These are very sturdy and durable threads that can be too thick to use in beading seed beads, but might be useful for attaching larger beads.

Nylon thread. There are several types of nylon thread available on the market. Nymo, one of the most commonly available styles, is very tough and makes an excellent basis for beaded fringe. You can find this thread at most bead stores.

Silk thread. Silk thread comes in a broad range of colors and in a number of different thicknesses. If you are using some very small beads, this can be a

good choice. The very fine thread will slip through even the smallest needle eye, or the tiniest hole in a bead. Silk thread is graded by letter, from A to F, with two finer sizes, 0 and 00.

Dental floss. Some dancers swear by dental floss for making beaded fringe because of its sheer strength. Some of the newer flosses are fine enough to pass through even the smallest bead. However, the color is limited to white, which might show up in a costume. Dental floss is very inexpensive and is widely available.

Other Supplies

Beeswax. One easy way to strengthen your thread and prevent it from twisting while you are working is to give it a coating of beeswax. Available at all beading shops and most craft and sewing stores, beeswax is an inexpensive tool that can streamline your stitching.

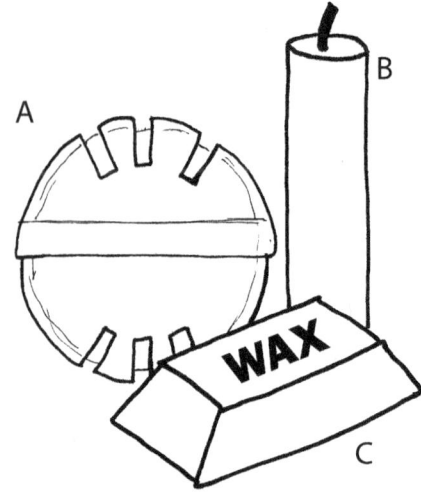

A: Thread wax holder.
B: Candle.
C: Beeswax cake.

To use beeswax, simply pull your thread tautly across the surface of the cake of wax. The thread will pick up the wax as it is dragged through. To make the thread pliable and soft, iron your waxed thread on a medium setting. This conditions the thread and makes it supple, strong, and less likely to twist and knot.

Embroidery hoops. Frames or hoops hold the fabric taut and provide an excellent stretched surface upon which to bead. Almost essential for making appliqués, the embroidery hoop will also come in handy when making beaded fringe on a tape. Embroidery hoops come in a variety of styles: plastic spring locking, wooden with a tension screw, and scroll type frames that allow large pieces of fabric to be mounted. Most types will work for making appliqués. Shapes can vary from the traditional round to rectangular or oval varieties. If you plan on doing a lot of beadwork, you might want to buy a large rectangular frame mounted on legs, which can be especially useful for tambour beading techniques.

Scissors. This may seem like an obvious item and one that you might already have in your toolbox. While you can get away with using a standard pair of sewing shears, having a small pair of tailors points, embroidery scissors, or even a thread clipper can be a handy help for clipping close to the source. This can be especially handy when clipping beside knots or when working in the middle of very complicated designs. Buy the best quality scissors you can afford and keep them protected so they will stay sharp and give you years of good service.

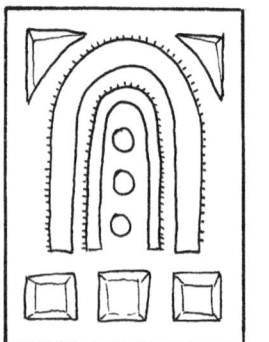

Beading Trays. Designed for jewelry makers, beading trays come in an assortment of styles and configurations. The most common style is made from plastic that has been flocked to give it a nice napped surface. This surface is critical, in that it prevents the beads from rolling around a lot. Most trays have a groove, cut in the shape of a necklace, with wells for placing loose beads. While these can be handy, they are poorly suited for the dance designer interested in doing beaded appliqués or embroidery.

Some designers like to create their own trays. One designer I know uses a shoebox lid lined with velvet. She has lids lined in black and gray to aid her while sorting and laying out beads of different colors. Another designer I have

Surface Embellishments

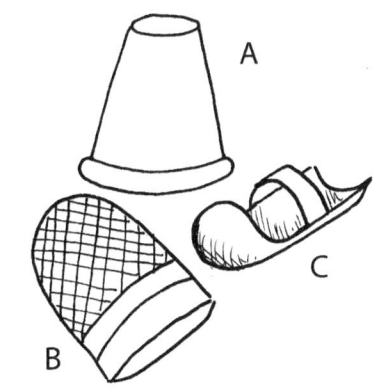

A: Standard thimble. B: Leather thimble.
C: Plastic thimble.

worked with uses a jewelry store display pallet. Again, this is covered with velvet, which holds the beads still. These types of display units are available from some bead suppliers.

Thimble. A good, well-fitted thimble is almost a requirement for doing beading. A thimble provides leverage and allows you to push even the finest needle. There are a wide variety of thimbles out on the market. Check not only in the notions department of your fabric store, but also where quilting supplies are sold. Always try on a thimble before purchase to test the fit.

Tweezers. These handy little tools can be quite helpful especially when placing small beads into complex designs. Bead shops sell a wide variety of shaped tweezers, some which close down around the bead like a clamp, holding it steady during positioning and even stitching.

Adhesive products. Adhesive products are useful for reinforcing knots and thread loops on the underside of cloth during the beading process. Make sure to use a clear, flexible glue designed for use on cloth. There is a more complete discussion of bead products in the following chapter.

Three adhesive products that are essential for the sewing box are fray check (for controlling the edges of fabric), standard fabric glue, and a glue stick with restickable or repositionable glue.

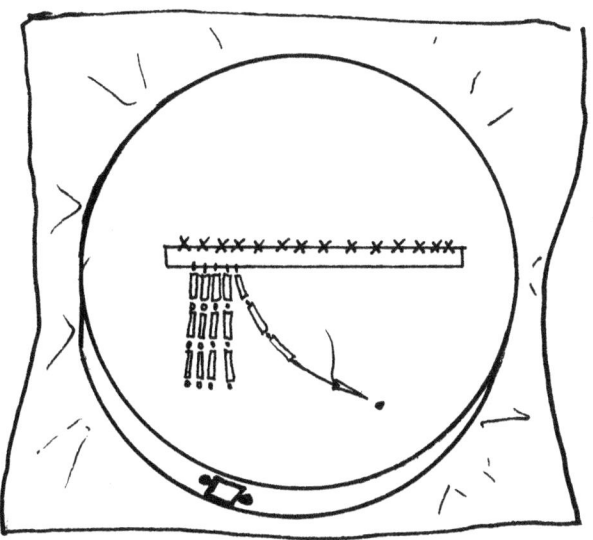

Embroidery hoop with fringe in progress. Fringe can be mounted on tape to allow ease of placement. An embroidery hoop makes this an easy project.

10 Beading Techniques

Elaborately beaded costumes are wonderfully complex, visual feasts for the eyes. Finding resources on beading techniques can be frustrating. Books on beading tend to focus on jewelry construction, leaving only a few scant pages devoted to embellishing cloth. Other books are encyclopedic, with directions for each specific stitch, but little information about how to use these techniques in a complete design.

In the world of crafts, the best directions for beaded fabric embellishments are listed not under beading, but bead embroidery. Here, you will find embroidery books contain limited useful information. Several books are currently in print with well-written chapters that focus on the techniques of beading. My favorite titles are listed in the beading section of the bibliography.

On the next few pages are illustrations and directions for my favorite beading stitches. Remember, virtually any embroidery stitch can be used in beading. Simply load up a suitable amount of seed beads and complete the stitch. The result will be a beaded version of the embroidery design. I recommend investing in a basic embroidery book that is well illustrated, with easy to follow directions.

Single Bead Stitch

The single bead stitch is probably the most basic of beading techniques. The thread comes from the back of the cloth. A bead is slipped over the needle and slid down the thread and seated against the cloth. A stitch is taken through the cloth to secure the bead, and then the process continues. This is a very secure stitch, especially if a knot is tied between each bead. This stitch is used in scatter beading and in areas that require precise bead placement.

Lazy Stitch

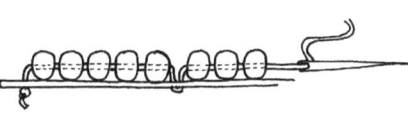

The lazy stitch covers a lot of territory more quickly than the single bead stitch. For this technique you may need a longer beading needle to stack up the beads. The beads are strung onto the thread, as many as eight seed beads can be applied in one stitch. Smooth the beads across the surface of the fabric, then take a stitch through the cloth and repeat. This technique can make straight lines or zigzag rows. This technique can also be worked as a fill stitch working back and fourth across the fabric rather than in a straight line.

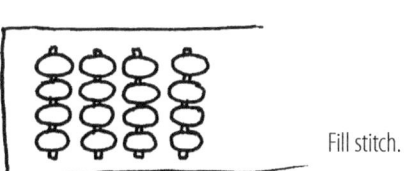

Fill stitch.

Side view of fill stitch.

Because the thread is only attached on the ends of the rows, the tension of the thread is critical. If you find the thread is too loose, and the beads are looping away from the cloth, go back into the stitching and use the couching stitch to secure the beads. If the thread is too tight, the fabric will begin to pucker beneath the rows of beads.

Couching

This technique uses two threads to attach the beads. The first thread holds a row of beads. The second thread is worked from beneath the fabric, coming up and catching the top thread at regular intervals to stitch the row of beads down. This technique can work well with larger beads such as pearls or faceted crystals.

Running Stitch/Back Stitch

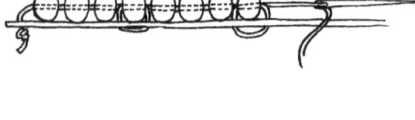

The backstitch is similar to the lazy stitch, except you use much shorter strands of beads, six or less. The row is laid across the fabric, making sure to control the tension so it's neither too tight nor too loose. When you take your next stitch through the cloth, go backwards and come back up between the last and second to the last bead. Loop back through the last bead. Continue forward with your next row. This is a very sturdy stitch especially if you knot frequently.

Chain Stitch

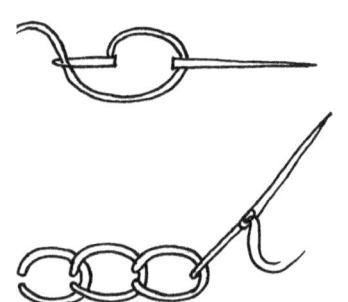

The chain stitch is used extensively in Indian embroidery. This is a beaded twist on a traditional embroidery design. The chain stitch is a looping stitch. To make a chain stitch, start as you would any embroidery stitch with the knot on the wrong side of the cloth. Make a loop with your thread and put your needle into the cloth next to where it appears from below. Pass the needle to the back of the cloth and then come out one "loop length" away. Continue as needed. To add beads to this stitch, make a sample to find out how many beads will fit on the loop. Use an even number of beads that will make balanced loops.

Other Embroidery Stitches

Other stitches that are effective when beading include the fly stitch, herringbone stitch, and needlepoint's continental stitch. Using an embroidery book as a guide, experiment with different stitches to use as filler for larger beading patterns. If you work as a seamstress, having a sampler or a sample book with different beaded stitches will serve as a reference for you as well as a marketing tool for clients. This book can become a source of inspiration for future projects and will help you get an idea of how long it takes for a particular stitch and how many beads are ideal.

Tips for Beadwork

- Wax your thread to prevent twisting.
- Plan your designs on paper before you begin.
- Take frequent breaks. Many beaders hunch over their work, so take the time to stretch your hands, neck, and back.
- Have a good light. A color-balanced light will give you a better idea of your color combinations and help prevent eyestrain.
- Buy the best tools you can afford. This will help save time and reduce the frustration of "making do."

Beading Techniques

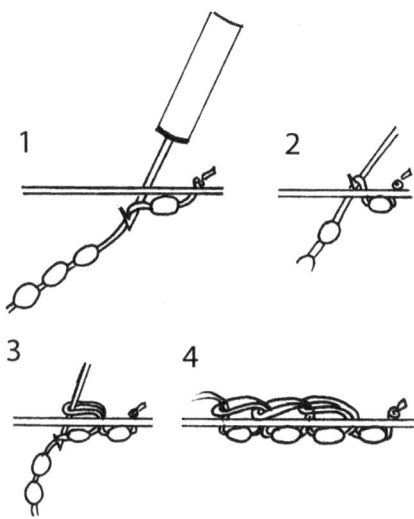

Tambour Beading

In this technique a special hooked tool, called a tambour, is used to stitch the beads from the reverse side of the cloth. The fabric is pulled tightly using an embroidery frame. A single thread is loaded with beads. The tambour is pushed through the fabric and a loop of the thread is pulled up through the cloth. Beads are then seated into position and the tambour is pushed through again, pulling the thread tight and securing the beads between stitches. On the reverse side, the stitch resembles the chain stitch. Because tambour beading requires two hands, one to manipulate the needle and the other to feed the beads below, a frame mounted on legs will leave both hands free to execute the stitches.

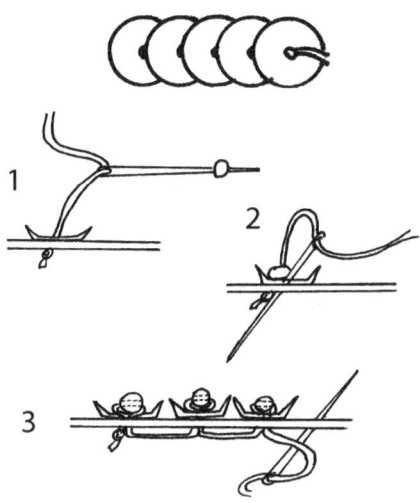

Sequins

Applying sequins is very similar to working with single beads. Since they are a flat disk, the can be layered on the cloth, building up a rich texture. Stitching them on one at time can create a different effect and reduce the number of beads required to cover the surface.

Flat Technique

To apply a flat sequin, you can use one of two techniques. The most common is to use a seed bead to secure the sequin to the cloth. Pass a thread up through the fabric and string a sequin and one bead. Pass the needle back through the sequin, pulling the bead down to hold the sequin in place. If you choose not to use a bead, you can stitch across the sequin to hold it in place.

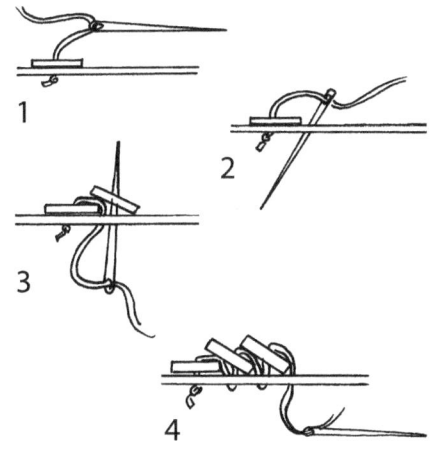

Layered Technique

This technique can create rows of sequins that can be formed in straight or curved lines. This technique can also be used with beads between the sequins to cause them to stand away from the cloth creating a more exaggerated texture. Pre-stitched sequins on strings are an inexpensive surface embellishment, and are manufactured using this format.

Begin by placing the first sequin on the cloth by passing a thread up through the center of the sequin and then stitching back through the fabric at the sequin's edge. Bring the thread up in the same location and place your sequin. Half of the first sequin, and the stitch used to hold it to the cloth, will be obscured by the second sequin. Repeat the stitch as needed.

Adhesive Products

Many dancers don't have the time or patience to make complicated beading, yet still want to use beads. An alternative to stitching beads is to use adhesives. Below is a list of types of adhesives that can be used to apply beads to the surface of cloth. Unfortunately, beads that are glued on, in general, aren't as sturdy and cannot stand up to abrasion as well as stitched beads. But adhesives can come in handy when doing repairs, for theme costumes that need to get done quickly, and for students or beginner costumes that will only be worn a few times. Some dancers craft very elaborate and beautiful costumes almost entirely using glue. Always test your adhesive products on all materials in your costume to check for discoloration, strength and durability.

Fabric Glue

This all-purpose adhesive is similar to the standard white school glues, except they have extenders and binders that adhere to porous cloth. There are many varieties of fabric glue, so when shopping look for adhesives that are washable and don't stiffen up. Fabric glue is good for lightweight beads, sequins, and trim.

Beading Glue

There are several brands of glue on the market designed specifically to adhere sequins and beads to cloth. Look for the words "gem" or "bead" on the packaging and read the fine print. Some will specify a maximum weight for the jewels. These glues can support larger pieces than standard fabric glue.

Fabric Paint

An alternate way to adhere gems and beads to cloth is to use an acrylic-based textile paint as a glue. There is a tremendous variety in fabric paints available at your local craft store. From puffy paint to metallic, mixing your own colors gives you an infinite number of possible colors to choose from. Paint can become part of the overall design or can act as a setting for your gems, producing a thin circle around the embellishment.

Epoxy

Favored by ballroom dancers to apply rhinestones to dresses, epoxy is super strong and works really well, no matter how sheer the fabric is. Epoxy can be toxic; use it in an area with good ventilation. Epoxy may not dry clear, so make sure not to use too much of this product or you could wind up with yellow halos around your embellishments.

Hot Glue

Avoid using hot glue on costumes. The heat of the body can release low-temp hot glue. Hot glue is stiff and brittle, and while it might be a good option for attaching a fabric accessory to a pin or clip, actually using it to attach gems and beads to cloth can create lumpy, stiff results. If you decide to use hot glue, pre-test all of your materials. Some synthetic cloth will melt or change color even when using a low-temperature gun.

Tips for Using Glue

Always use a tray. This makes it easy to use small implements such as toothpicks.

Clear a drying area for your costume before you begin.

Always make a test sample to ensure that the products won't cause the beads or cloth to bleed or peel.

Hand Beading Fringe

Beading fringe can be a time consuming process, but is often worth the effort to get exactly what you want. When you have more time than cash, hand beading offers the option of creating a designer costume with a small financial investment in materials and supplies. Be realistic about the amount of time it will require when you are designing a costume. Making hand beaded fringe will go faster if you use larger beads. Rocailles, while lovely, will take endless hours to string, especially if you are trying to mimic the effect of Egyptian style fringe. Compare the cost of pre-made Egyptian fringe against the cost of materials to create the same effect. You may find that purchasing commercial fringe is worth the savings in time.

Strands

From a construction point of view, strand beads are the most time consuming and tricky. The thread passes through each strand of beads twice. First, the thread passes through all of the beads to the very end. Then you skip the last bead, and slip your needle through all of the beads in the row on your way back up to the top. The bottom bead serves as a lock, holding the strand in place.

Strands can be made in varying lengths to create a shaped hem. The strands can be composed of several styles of beads. For instance, by varying the color of your beads, you can create decorative designs in the fringe. By using different styles of beads, rocailles and bugles for example, you can create pattern by contrasting the textures.

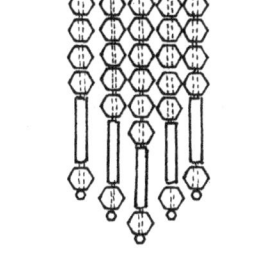

Looped Fringe

The structure of this style of fringe is similar to a swag and yet gives a look that approximates strand fringe. In this style, the thread is passed through the row of beads and is pulled up and knotted at the top. The loop is made quite small so as to create the illusion of two closely spaced strands of beads. Because you are only going through the row of beads once, this is a faster method of creating a lot of fringe. Make sure to load twice as many beads as the desired length of the fringe. A knot between each loop will ensure you won't loose a whole row of beading if the thread breaks.

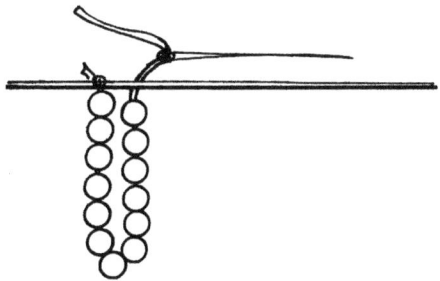

 Design fringe using the beading template in the appendix.

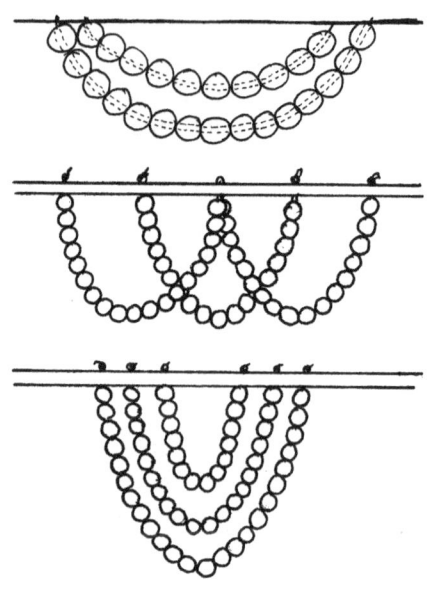

Swags

These can really pull the eye around a costume with swoops of color and texture. Swags are a speedy way of getting a lot of impact while minimizing the amount of time spent working on the beads. Unlike strand fringe, swags can use much larger beads. If you are going for size and volume, consider the weight of the beads and opt for lighter plastic styles rather than glass or stone. Swags are made by loading a row of beads onto a thread, looping it loosely a distance away from the start, and then stitching it down onto the costume. Swags can be effectively combined with loops and strands to create complex arrangements of beads. Single strands can also be dropped from swags, adding a further dimension to your decorative trim.

Adding a drop to a swag

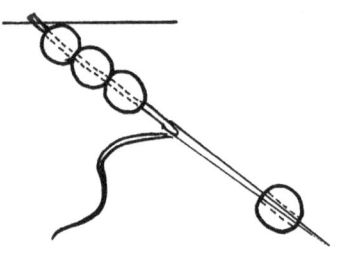

Step 1: Load half the beads onto your thread.

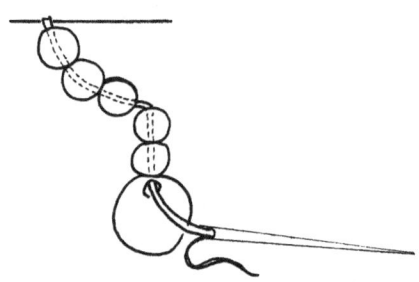

Step 2: Slip the beads from the drop portion onto the thread.

💡 Attaching fringe to a twill tape band will make the piece of fringe easy to move and recycle.

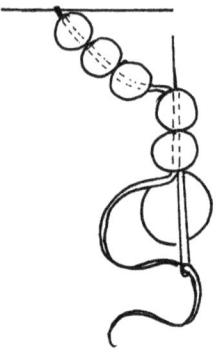

Step 3: Go back through the drop beads.

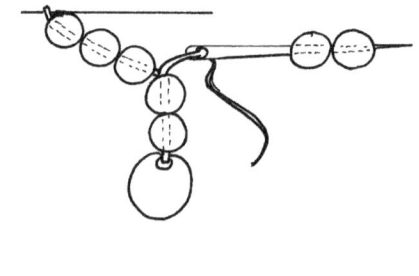

Step 4: Continue with the swag, loading more beads and sewing to the cloth.

Clusters

Made from either strands or loops, clusters of beads can replace the traditional length of fringe. Clusters can be dropped from the edge of a garment or from a planned surface embellishment or design. A cluster of strands or loops can save a lot of time and money by focussing the beads only where they are needed, creating the illusion of a tassel. Clusters can also be used judiciously to draw the eye to specific locations and can be used to create focal points. Make sure that the fabric that clusters are mounted on is reinforced because a cluster will put a lot of tension in one small area of the cloth.

11 Developing Beaded Designs

Radial scatter beading.

There are two major ways to apply beaded designs to your costumes. Dancers with limited time can invest in pre-made beaded and sequined appliqués that can quickly be stitched into place on the bedlah. Appliqués provide a convenient way to match a group of costumes in a troupe situation where the sewing skills of the members vary. The other option is to bead directly on the cloth of the bra and belt. This can produce very sturdy and beautiful results. Unlike the appliqué technique, you don't have to deal with a limited selection of colors and patterns, or the awkward and unsightly edges.

The actual process of beading is the same in both techniques, although making an appliqué requires a bit more preparation of the cloth. But regardless of what you are beading on, coming up with the pattern is the next step. In this chapter, I will offer some ideas for developing designs for beading.

Geometric Patterns

Geometric patterns are the easiest to bead. The regular shape of the bead and the repetition of an organized repetitive pattern make them easy for beginners to follow. Unlike complex floral and other representational imagery, geometric patterns require less focussed concentration, allowing an experienced beader to let her fingers fly over the piece. Here are a few ways to develop geometric patterns for use in your beadwork.

Scatter beading. While this may not sound like a geometric beading technique, scatter beading can be used to develop loosely formed patterns. In scatter beading, the beads and other surface embellishments are applied to the surface of the cloth in a seemingly random pattern. The scatter technique is especially effective with bugle beads. Lines can wiggle across the surface of the cloth in a specific direction or radiate outward from a central point.

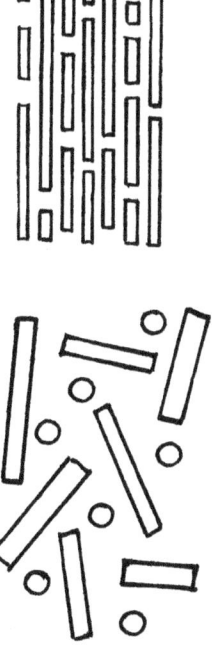

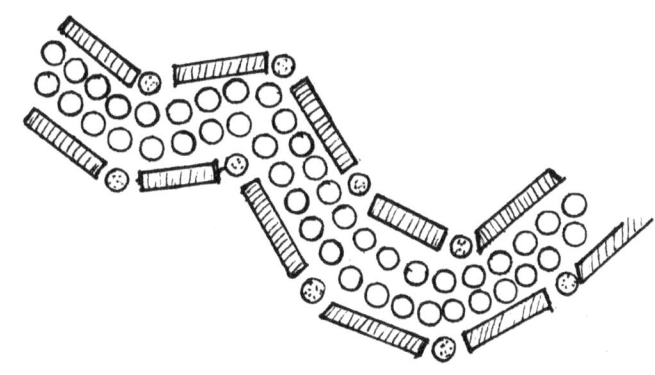
Scatter beading examples.

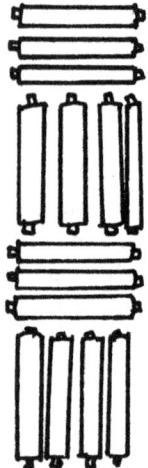

Geometric patterns. When using bugle beads, it's easy to form repeatable geometric patterns by utilizing the nature of the bead shape. This can be especially effective with combinations of bead styles and sizes. Play with your beads. Lay them out on a piece of cloth and start arranging and rearranging them into patterns. Think about designs you have seen in brick or tile work and see if you can recreate them in beads.

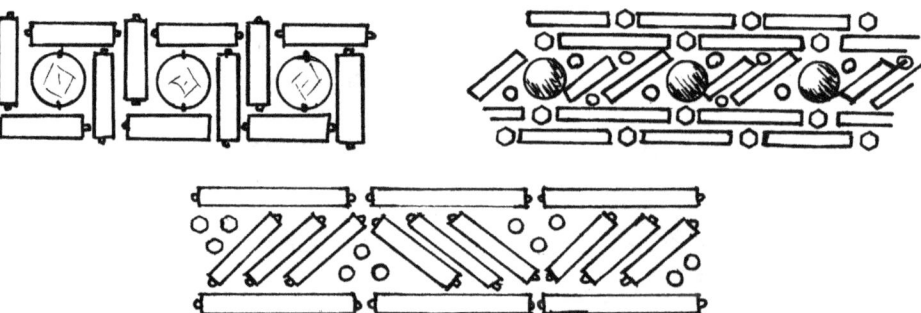

Following designs. Patterned fabric, lace, or trim can be a good source for beaded designs. If your bedlah is covered with a patterned fabric, you can select part of the pattern to follow with the beads. You can select specific areas to emphasize with the beading. You can fill in areas or trace lines across the cloth. Beading allows you to integrate color and texture, adding another dimension to the cloth.

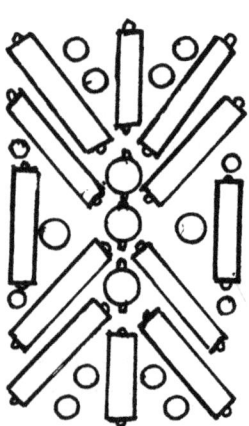

Using Clip Art

Clip art is the easiest foundation on which to create designs for beadwork. There are hundreds of clip art sources, from books to CDROM collections. The images are generally clean line art that can be easily transformed and manipulated to build complex designs. In this section, I will share my approach to using clip art, step-by-step. You can use these techniques to develop patterns for your own beading projects.

There are many other sources for inspiration for beaded designs. Fine art books focussing on Islamic art can provide a wealth of images from which to build beading motifs and designs. Artworks from the Orientalist movement, with Westernized fantasies of an imagined Middle East, can be very inspirational for costume designers, not only for their designs but for the lush imagery and color. But for this method, I prefer to start with clean line art.

Developing Beaded Designs

Select the Design

Look for an image that fits the theme of your costume. In general, beaded designs become the focal point of the costume. There is a wealth of imagery available. Select designs that are personally meaningful for you. From flowers to geometrics, there are thousands of motifs to choose from. If you are planning on investing in a book of clip art, look for one with a wide variety of appealing and useful images.

For the examples used in this section, I have chosen three motifs from a Dover book entitled *Decorative Flower and Leaf Designs.* The first is a swirling paisley image, the second features a stylized basket of flowers, while the third is a hybrid of the first two. I selected these three images because I like undulating flow of the outlines of the shapes and the smooth curves of the figures.

Clip art examples.

Altering the Images

When you have chosen the images to serve as the basis for your designs, the next step is to play with the motifs, altering them to fit the needs of your costume. Decide where the designs will be located on the finished costume. What shapes are the spaces and how big are they? You may need to enlarge or reduce the sizes of the images. One single design motif can be manipulated in a variety of ways to create an entire matching ensemble.

Take your clip art book to a copy center and have numerous copies made of your image. Make sure you have an ample supply, because you will be cutting and pasting. Copy them in a variety of different sizes and, if you can, flip some of the designs to make mirror images. Having the finished design in the final size will make laying out the beads a much easier process.

If you discover an image is too complicated to paint with beads and sequins, you can eliminate some of the nonessential lines. This can be a very important step, especially if you are shrinking the image. Take a clean photocopy of the image and use a whiteout pen to erase some of the smaller interior details.

A whiteout pen has been used to simplify the design.

Cut and Paste

Once you have your copies made, carefully cut the pieces out. Lay them across a table and just look at them, contemplating how they can effectively interlock. Mix them up, pairing off different sizes, and develop alternate configurations. Using the three motifs, these are some of the patterns that I came up with.

Clusters. Simple repetitive grouping of the same motif can create an interesting cluster effect. Try using the motif in different orientations, rotating them and flipping them to create visual intersections where the designs meet.

Pairs in opposition. Here, I took the same motif and pairing it with its own kind, both rotated and flipped, to create two alternative looks that would work well over the cups of a bra.

Multiple motifs. Combining two different motifs will expand the options. In this design, suitable for a triangular shaped belt, I've taken mirror images of the paisley and paired them with the flower urn pattern.

Combining altered versions. In the next design, I have used three versions of the flower urn pattern, but the central image has had some of the decoration removed to simplify the design and make it fit the shape of the costume better.

Trace the Design

When you have settled on your patterns, the last step is to carefully trace your pattern. This tracing will remove any non-essential lines, resulting in a very graphic linear design. Using this tracing as a guide, lay out your beads within the design. I like to draw the beads in and then color them with a pencil to specify placement. When you have perfected your design, transfer it to cloth using fabric tracing paper. Now you are ready to begin the process of beading.

The finished beating template.

Part III
Completing the Look

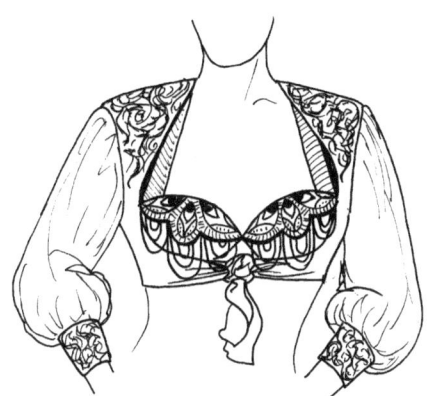

The last part of the book is an overview of all of the garments and accessories that support and accentuate the bra and belt set. Since bedlah is worn without a skirt or pants, it becomes another kind of costume, transforming the oriental dancer into a showgirl. The bra and belt cannot stand alone, so in the following chapters I have created a portfolio of popular garment styles. There are hundreds of items to choose from when you are designing a complete ensemble, from costume essentials, such as skirts and pants, to accent and accessories.

This, hopefully, will serve as a source of inspiration for your design work. As you examine the pictures and read the descriptions of these garments, think of how you can put these pieces to work for you. Consider the lines and shapes of the garments and how each piece can draw the viewer's eye to your most outstanding features. Alternately, keep your eyes opened for garments that might help minimize the problem areas.

Chapter 12 introduces the main themes in skirt and pant designs popular among dancers today. Subsequent chapters present other important garments. In Chapter 13, various styles of accent garments such as vests, blouses, hip wraps and over skirts are presented along with ideas on how to integrate these garments into complete ensembles. Chapter 14 explores the options for dresses and gowns that can either support or even replace the bra and belt set. And no ensemble would be complete without a few finishing accessories, which can be found in Chapter 15.

Part III forms a lexicon of design ideas that can spark your imagination. When you look at a style, contemplate the possibilities. Think of options in fabrics, surface design treatments, beading, and appliqués; the options are limitless. Consider how you can change interior lines or exterior shapes. Experiment by drawing various pieces together on a stock figure to help you visualize complete looks.

12 Skirts and Pants

Skirts and pants can be paired. Here, the skirt is lifted to reveal the pants below.

Perhaps no other garment in the dancer's wardrobe comes in as many shapes and styles as the skirt. From loose flowing styles to tightly fitted sheaths, there is a skirt option to flatter every body shape. There are only a few basic skirt shapes. However, there are a myriad of subtle permutations. If you find the number of style options overwhelming, stop and ask yourself a few questions to determine what you need in a skirt style:

Do I spin a lot during my dance? If the answer is yes, you might want to pick one of the fuller flowing styles such as the classic, tiered, or gored skirts. If you don't want to play up spins, there are numerous straight skirt styles that might be right for you.

Do I do floor work? Some skirts don't lend themselves to ease of floor work. Straight styles that are highly fitted, or limit leg movement, might not be an ideal choice. Fuller skirts might be a better selection for your performance needs.

Do I play with my skirt? For dancers who like to pick up their skirt and use it as a prop in their dance, fuller styles such as the tiered, gored, or circular skirt might be the best option. Most straight skirts do not lend themselves to skirt manipulation during performances.

Do I want to de-emphasize my hips? The shape of the skirt has a direct impact on the amount of visual attention directed towards the hips. Form-fitting skirts will emphasize the hip region by fitting tightly through the thighs. Tiered skirts will also emphasize the hips if they are cut with excess fullness that adds bulk at the waistline. Straight skirts that drop from the hip, or fuller skirts that are sleekly fitted across the hip region and gradually flare to the hem, are good choices if this is a design issue for you.

 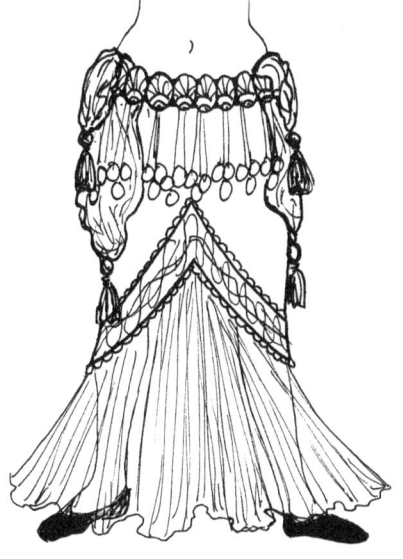

The Classic

Worn by dancers for more than half a century, the classic three-panel dance skirt is a time- tested style that can be a beautiful and flowing addition to any performer's wardrobe. This style of skirt is constructed from three half-circle panels. Two panels are stitched together to form the back of the skirt. The front panel is allowed to swing free, creating two long openings that expose the dancer's legs. These skirts can be made from chiffon or georgette for a soft and sheer look. Silk charmeuse or crepe-backed satin are more opaque alternatives that drape and flow beautifully in this style.

An alternative to the classic is a closed circle skirt. This style is also made from half-circle panels but they are stitched closed. Three, four, and up to eight panels can be stitched together creating an extremely full skirt style. This style of skirt can look good with virtually any costume style from tribal to glamorous bedlah.

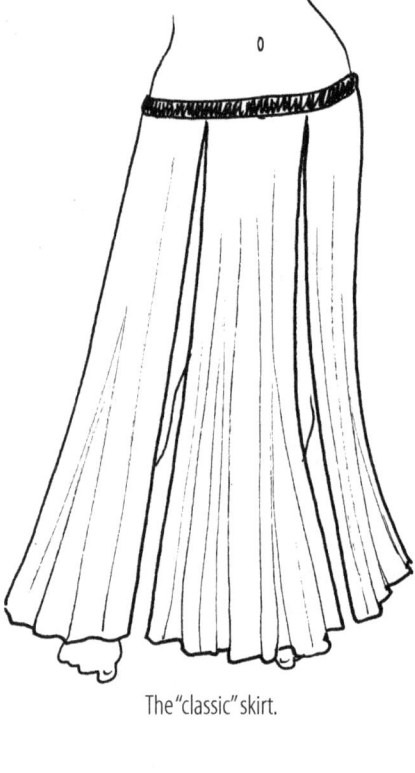

The "classic" skirt.

Variation: six panels stitched closed.

Variation: four panels stitched with flounce.

The Tiered Skirt

A favorite of Gypsy-fusion, tribal, and historical dancers is the tiered skirt. Made from long strips of cloth gathered and stitched together, the tiered skirt is one of the easiest, if time-consuming, skirt styles to make. While three tiers is the most popular and common format available from vendors, tiered skirts can be made with any number of rows. When made from very crisp fabric such as cotton, this style of skirt will really create a full hemline. Lighter weight fabrics create a softer shape with less fullness throughout. Check the latest fashion trends. Occasionally, tiered skirts come into style and can be purchased readymade and used for practice or performance.

Multi-tiered skirt.

Three-tiered skirt.

The Straight Skirt

Currently very popular among designers, the straight skirt is a cost-effective garment due to its smaller yardage requirements. Shaped hemlines, slits, ruffles, and decorative panels create visual interest and change the silhouette of the skirt. Dancers who are interested in creating a long lean line can turn to the straight skirt for body skimming styles. For dancers trying to downplay the width of their hips, a straight skirt should fall freely from the hipline to prevent the skirt from clinging through the thighs. Straight skirts made from fabric containing Spandex will cling, accentuating the thigh and hip region.

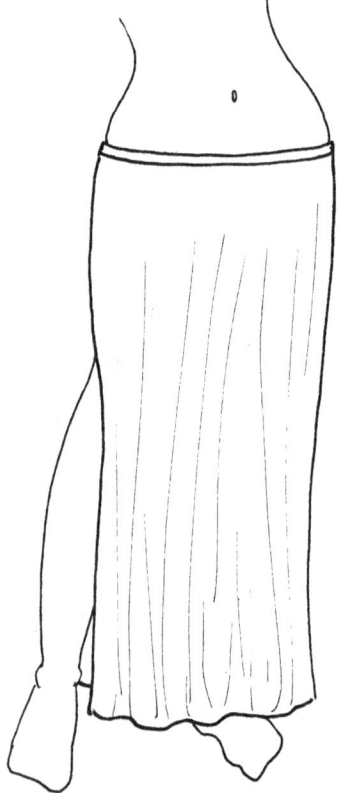
Straight skirt with deep chiffon ruffle.

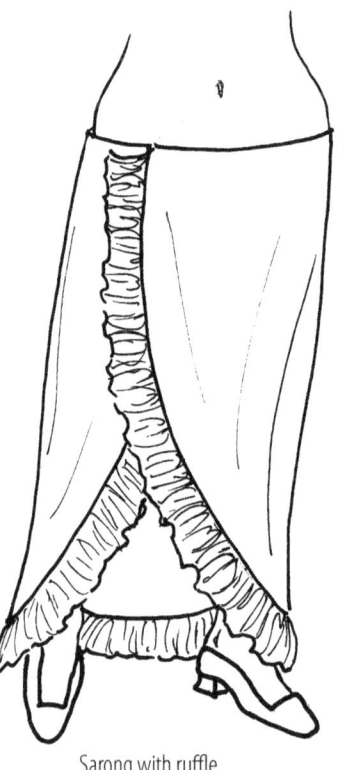
Sarong with ruffle.

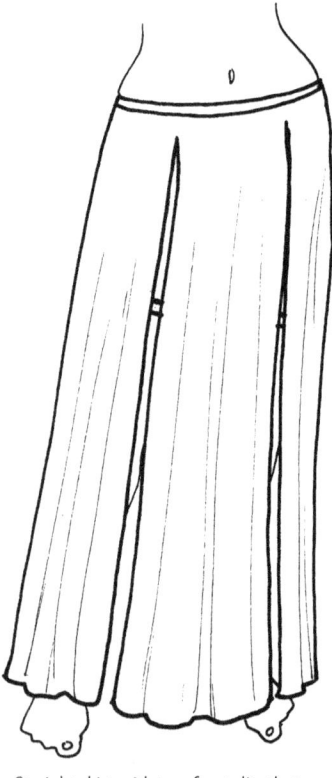
Straight skirt with side slits.

Straight skirt with two front slits that mimic the "classic."

Skirts and Pants

Gored Skirts

These skirts are smooth and body skimming, from hip to the knee, with fullness created below the knee down by the shaping of the skirt panels. Gored skirts come in a variety of different styles. While the six-gored skirt is the most popular, there are several different variations that use as many as twelve panels. One exciting variation of the gored skirt has curved panels that form a swirl that ripples down the body. A tip for dancers who are interested in experimenting with gored skirts: look at patterns for formal wear, especially bridal wear. Many dresses feature gored skirts. Simply ignore the bodice pieces, lower the waistline to your hips, and add a hip band.

Standard gored skirt.

Gored swirl skirt.

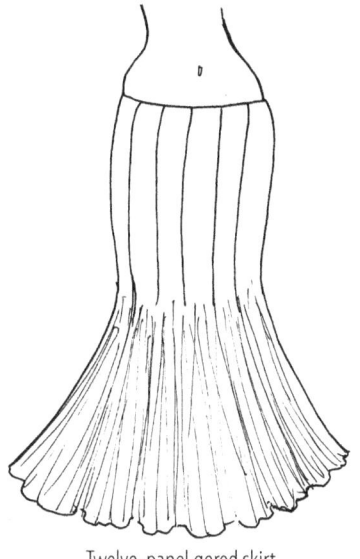

Twelve-panel gored skirt.

Godets

This style of skirt is made from a rectangle of fabric that's slit to the knee or thigh region. Small triangles or half-circle pieces are stitched into these slits to create additional fullness at the hem. When made from contrasting fabric, the panels become highlighted as a design feature. The size and shape of the godets can vary according to your stylistic needs. If you like a straight skirt style, small wedge-shaped godets can add just enough width for ease of movement. For a fuller skirt, add taller godets around the hem in regular intervals. A single godet can be added at the center back to allow the dancer to move but, unlike a slit, it conceals the legs.

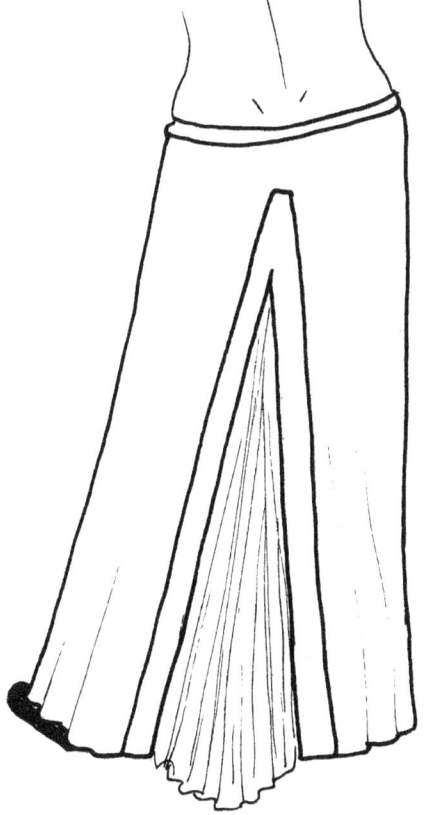

Single, large godet, replaces back slit.

Godet with lace panels.

Pants

The traditional Arabic word for pants is salwar. Traditionally, there have been three major styles of pants: harem pants with a shaped crotch seam and gathered ankles, gusseted pants with a wide deep central gusset, and draped pants where crotch shaping is created with added width at the center seam.

While pants are not essential for the bedlah costume, they can offer a refreshing change from the skirt. Pants are a versatile item that can become a workhorse in the dance ensemble. They can be worn alone with a belt, with a skirt topper, or paired with a skirt. For dancers who are looking for complete coverage and security, opaque pants will conceal the legs completely from view. For performers who wear full skirts or dance on a raised stage, pants can prevent the audience from unintentional glimpses of forbidden sights.

Many costuming styles utilize pants as part of their formula. Tribal dancers wear brightly colored pants under their full, tiered skirts. When they spin, their skirts flip and fly, revealing a shock of color to the audience. Dancers who do a lot of floor work can rely on pants to keep their legs covered and help protect their knees. For troupes, coordinating or matching pants can be an effective way of unifying a set of unrelated costume pieces.

There are fewer styles of pants out there than there are skirts. Because of the nature of the body and the need for a shaped crotch seam, pants can be a little more complicated to stitch together. Fortunately, most styles can be adapted from commercial patterns or drafted from measurements of the body.

Skirts and Pants

Harem Style Pants

Perhaps the most basic and common style is the harem pant. Harem pants are very similar to pants made for contemporary athletic wear. A commercial pattern for sweat pants can be cut down to the hip line, transforming them into a pair of narrow harem pants. For fuller styles, simply add width at the side seam. For more pouf at the ankle, add length. Slits, cuffs, yokes, and applied surface embellishments can be used to really punch up a plain pair of harem pants.

Turkish Style Pants

These pants are popular throughout all of the regions that were once under Ottoman rule and lands beyond. This style is most commonly associated with African garments that are based on centuries old shapes and construction techniques. This style is traditionally custom made from the measurements of your body. These pants are composed of two pieces, one for the leg and one for the gusset. There are patterns for several variations of this style available from Folkwear patterns.

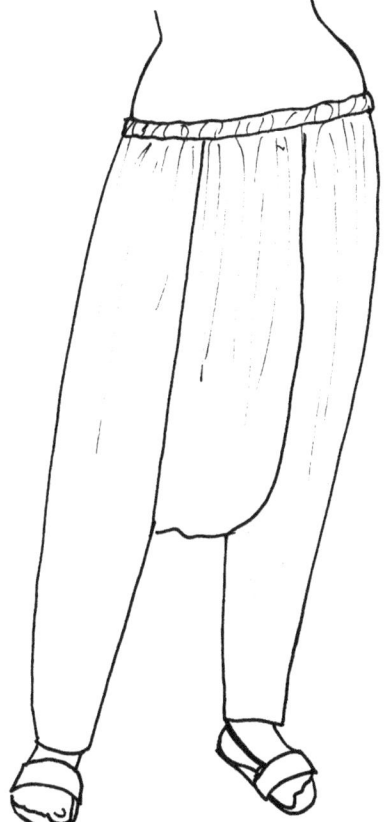

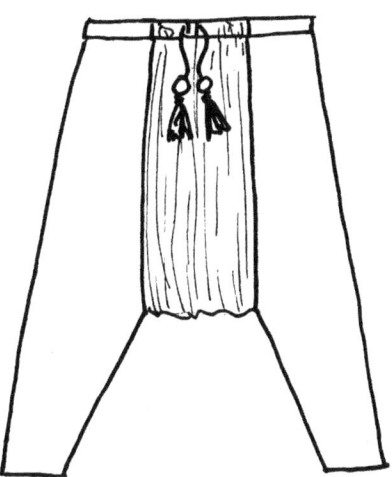

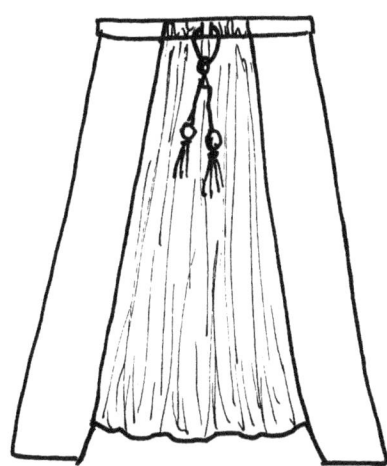

Turkish style pants with center gusset.   Turkish pants with tapered hem.   North African style pants with deep gusset to ankle.

Indian Style Pants

Indian-styled pants have a low deep crotch and narrow legs. Available in some Indian communities as part of the two-piece *salwar* and *camise* ensemble, these pants are comfortable and easy to stitch from a one-piece pattern developed from body measurements. The long, narrow legs can be fitted to the calf or extended longer to bunch at the ankles. Decorative or contrasting cuffs can make an interesting embellishment for this style of pants.

Indian pants with border print.

Salwar laid flat.

Indian salwar with long legs.

Other Styles

There are lots of other styles that can be transformed into stylish and sophisticated dance pants. Check out the more dressy designer styles in upscale pattern books for pants that might work for costuming purposes. Some styles, with angular draping, pegged tops, or shaped hems might make distinctive dancewear when constructed from fancy fabrics. Leggings, a comfortable alternative, can be embellished to make them performance-ready.

Draped pants with fullness at outseam.

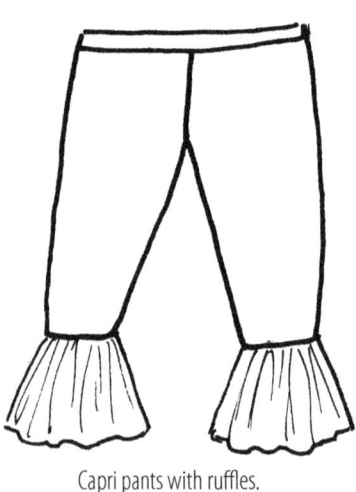
Capri pants with ruffles.

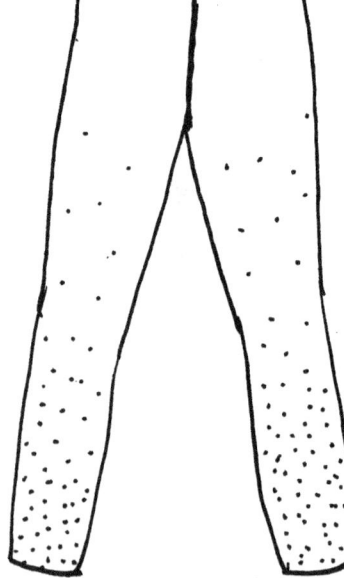
Embellished leggings.

13 Accent Garments

Accent garments aren't a necessity for your costume ensemble, but they can add an exciting layer of color, texture, and pattern. Bedlah can be mixed and matched with a wide variety of costume pieces beyond the basic skirt or pants. Having an assortment of coordinating accent garments can multiply the number of costume looks you can create with one bedlah set. Accent garments provide you with the ability to expand the dance wardrobe with less of an investment in time and money.

Troupes find that by using coordinated accent garments they can pull together unrelated bra and belt sets. This can be especially effective if the dancers are all using a basic color bedlah set, such as silver or gold, combined with a base color like black or red. Accent pieces can also help create a more unified look for troupes where the members all have different fitting and figure issues.

For designers working within tight budgetary constraints who are looking for ways to extend their wardrobe, accent garments are a perfect solution. Many of these items are small and can be made with scraps or remnants. Very expensive fabrics that a designer loves, but cannot afford for a bigger garment, can shine in a smaller accent piece. Even if you only have basic sewing skills, you can easily make accent garments from simple rectangles or you can modify patterns you can get at your local fabric store.

Coordinating your accent pieces is easy. You can match your costume by using the same fabrics, trims, and materials that you used to create your bedlah. By integrating the same lines, shapes, and details throughout all of your pieces you will instantly tie them together. Using the same edge treatments such as zigzags, swooping curves, or graceful arabesques will help create an integrated ensemble. A matching vest, overskirt, and veil will serve as a foundation ensemble for a variety of bra and belt sets.

Alternately, the accent garments can match each other. This will allow a dancer to wear this accent ensemble with a variety of different bedlah sets. When accent garments and accessories match, a very plain and simple bedlah set will be framed and supported, giving the dancer a more exciting and finished look.

Accent pieces add texture and pattern and can completely change the look of an ensemble. In this outfit, a tie blouse and handkerchief skirt topper punch up a plain bra and belt.

Vests

The vest is an exciting accent garment option derived from the styles popularly worn in the 19th century and imported to the United States with the first dancers. The vest can be adapted from vest patterns available from specialty dance and commercial pattern companies. There are many options in neckline and hem shape that can be achieved with slight modifications to the pattern. Make sure to sew a sample garment to test the cut and fit of the pattern before constructing the vest from expensive materials.

Bolero Style

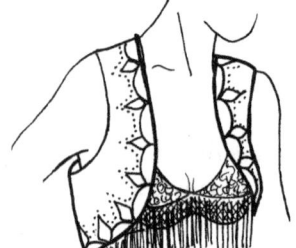

These vests are not designed to close. They frame the bra with smooth graceful curves that slide from neckline to hem. Patterns for bolero style vests are almost always available from commercial pattern companies, although they may be part of a suit or formal wear ensemble. To adapt for dance use, raise the hemline to either fall mid-torso or below the bust and reshape the curve of the front opening.

Turkish Style

These vests have swooping curves that wrap around the bra, curve below the bust, and close in the center beneath the bustline. Patterns for Turkish-style vests are available from vendors who specialize in dance costumes. This style of vest can look very good with a wide variety of costume styles, from high-glamour to historic and more. See the resources list in the appendices for pattern suppliers.

Laced Front

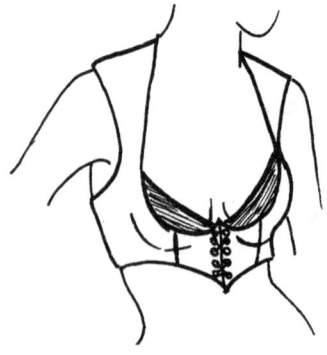

This style is essentially a shortened version of a European lady's bodice. This style has been worn since the Middle Ages by women around the Mediterranean. These vests look particularly good when worn with a loose, flowing blouse and can replace the bra when made to cover the bust. There are many vendors for historical patterns, including commercial pattern companies. Shorten the laced bodice and reshape the neckline to suit your style and taste. This is a good accent piece for Gypsy, Flamenco, historical, and vintage style ensembles.

Choli

There are two major stylistic groups of the choli. The traditional style is made from woven fabric and is fitted through the use of seaming. It ties at back and is based on centuries-old garment shapes from India. A contemporary stylistic variation is the stretch choli, which is made from fabric that is manufactured with Spandex. Stretch versions also cut below the bust but generally have a closed back. The choli is a great idea for dancers with ample bustlines who are searching for alternatives to the bra.

Traditional Indian-Style Choli

Traditional cotton or silk tie back choli are popular with tribal and historical dancers. When made from other fabrics you can transform the look, even while maintaining a more traditional line. A choli can be a great option for a dancer who acquires a belt that does not match its bra and wants to develop a cohesive costume. A choli and matching skirt will develop a unified look.

Contemporary Indian Stylized Choli

The contemporary Indian fashion industry produces choli designs that are innovative and sexy, with style lines that work beautifully for dancewear. If there are Indian stores in your area, stop and shop for ideas, if not for the garments themselves. Developing a pattern for this style might be a bit more difficult. If you shop the pattern catalogs, look for empire waist dresses that can be adapted by removing skirts and raising waistlines.

Stretch Choli

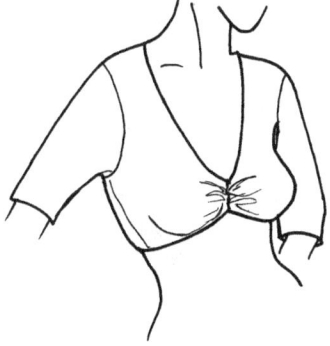

There are many Middle Eastern dance vendors who carry stretch cholis. Crop tops can also be purchased from general dance costume suppliers who sell jazz costumes and workout wear. When made from luxurious stretch velvet, the stretch choli can move out of the dance class and onto the performance stage. An easy stretch choli pattern can be made by cutting a standard bodysuit pattern below the bust and adding a band of elastic to the bottom edge.

Blouses

The blouse offers more coverage than the bra. When worn with a bra or vest, the blouse can offer the designer an opportunity to add a new texture and color to the top half of the ensemble. In addition, the blouse makes a very comfortable piece for practice and exercise. Many new dancers turn to the blouse as an inexpensive first performance costume piece. Unlike a choli, the blouse has a closed back and is loose-fitting, giving more coverage through the back, upper arms, and shoulders.

Peasant Blouse

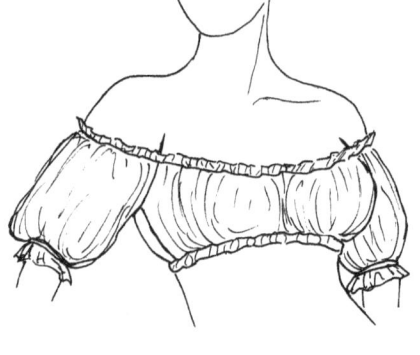

This style of blouse is perfect for achieving a historic Gypsy-styled look. These raglan-sleeved blouses are worn with either long or short sleeves. They gather at the neckline, under the bust, and at the hems of the sleeves. Every year around Halloween, pattern companies offer costume styles that include these blouses. Look for patterns that feature pirate or fantasy Gypsy ensembles.

Tie-Front Blouse

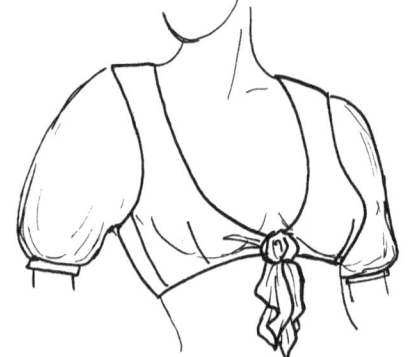

The tie-front blouse has a neckline that scoops under the bustline. This style frames the bra or can be cut to cover the bust and provides coverage of the arms, shoulders, and upper back. This is an excellent style for dancers who are looking for a garment that helps minimize exposure of these areas while maximizing the attention paid to the chest region. Any blouse pattern can be adapted for this purpose. Re-cut the neckline to the desired shape and remove the bottom half of the blouse. When shopping patterns, buy a style with a beautiful shoulder line and sleeves.

Peasant blouse with vest.

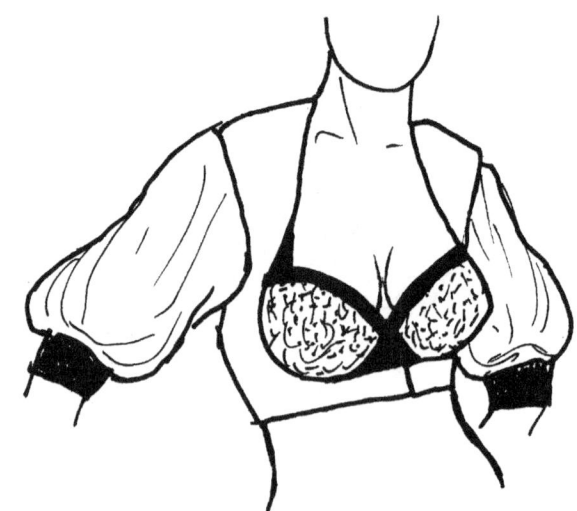

Blouse with bra.

Hip Wraps

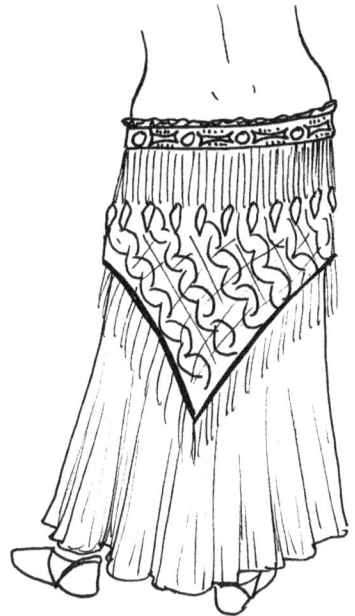

The addition of a simple hip wrap worn under the belt can transform the design of an ensemble. A simple skirt and belt can be punched up with color, texture, and an infusion of new design lines with the addition of a hip wrap. Adding fringe or tabs to the hip wrap increases the amount of potential movement. The number of items that can be used as a hip wrap is limited only by your imagination. Here is a short list with some ideas to help you start thinking of the possibilities.

Shawls

A simple black lace shawl with fringe, or a more elegant beaded wrap, can be used as the layer between the skirt and the belt. Shawls are available from most major department stores, and more formal styles are encrusted with beads or made from luxurious fabrics. These are available in many clothing shops, especially around the holidays. Look in stores that specialize in formal wear, wedding dresses, or even wearable art.

The Square or Triangle

Possibly the easiest costume piece to make is a square or triangle of dramatic exciting fabric to wear under the belt. From burn-out velvet to re-embroidered lace, a simple square can be made from materials too delicate, expensive, or brightly-patterned for use in a head-to-toe costume. Just measure your hips and make the square or triangle big enough to tie around your hips. A rule of thumb is to measure your hips and add at least 15 inches (40 cm) to allow enough length to tie a knot. This measurement goes on the diagonal of the square. If you don't like the unsightly appearance of a large knot, you can apply a hook and eye to the square allowing the ends hang loose.

Shaped and Trimmed Hip Wrap

Taking the square or triangle concept one step further, a decorative edge trim, row of fringe, or appliquéd design can add additional texture and movement. A triangular hip wrap can be reversible, multiplying the design possibilities of a single garment. The shape of the hem can dramatically change the look of the hip wrap. If you have a repeated motif throughout the bra and belt, you can translate these designs into a central appliqué or hem shape on a coordinated hip wrap.

Overskirts

Unusual, flirty, and fun overskirts can be a costume wardrobe stretcher. Overskirts can be made out of the same fabric as the bra and belt, or out of a dramatic fabric that will accentuate or harmonize with other garments. An overskirt in a color that is basic to your wardrobe can be mixed or matched with many bra and belt sets.

Overskirts are also a budget-friendly way of expanding your wardrobe. Think of the many possible ways you can integrate scraps or small remnants of leftover fabric. Stretch your budget dollar by using smaller pieces of very expensive material. You can coordinate overskirts with other accent pieces. A bra-framing vest worn with an overskirt of matching cloth can instantly coordinate an ensemble.

Tabs

The tabbed overskirt adds lots of movement to the costume and is essential for creating a late 19th century look. The tabs can be skinny, wide, or a mixture of both. The tabs can be the same length or varied to create asymmetrical interest. They can be widely spaced, or tightly packed like fringe. Fabric can vary from tab to tab, or they can be all the same. Make sure that you make an attractive lining for your tabs because when they flip and fly, the audience will be able to see the insides.

Handkerchief Style

Handkerchief skirts are made from a square of cloth with a circle cut in the middle to create a waistline. Handkerchief styles can be worn layered, with the points turned. Handkerchief styles require a square of fabric, buy the same length as your fabric width. So if your fabric is 44" wide, buy a 44" length. Handkerchief styles can even be a short revealing skirt for the adventurous dancer.

Panels

A pair of single decorative panels can be worn as either a very revealing skirt or layered over a full skirt as an accent garment. A panel accent skirt can be made from a single yard of cloth cut lengthwise and hemmed. Because of the smaller size, this accent skirt can be made from expensive cloth and worn over a fuller, less expensive skirt. Panels can also come in other shapes. From triangular points to swooping curves, the panel overskirt can integrate into the full ensemble by repeating design elements in their shapes.

14 Dresses

A dress is an excellent option for the dancer interested in a more covered look. A beautiful gown with decorative surface embellishments can be an independent garment that can replace the bedlah set. A very sleek and fitted dress can become a base garment to wear under a bra and belt. There are many styles of dresses available from commercial pattern companies that are perfectly suited for transforming into Middle Eastern dance wear.

There are several approaches to using dresses for developing costume ensembles within the costume wardrobe. Dresses are chameleon garments that can provide layering options. No matter what your style, from high glamour to quazi-historical, there is a dress style available for you. Here are a few ways you can put dresses to work in your wardrobe.

Bra and Belt Worn On Top

In this type of ensemble, the dress serves as an under-layer. Your bra and belt need to fit well over a dress. Lighter weight fabrics that stretch are ideal for this style. Some examples include stretch velvets, stretch lace, or a long, sleek, fitted dress constructed out of a lightweight silky material.

Dress with embellished bodice, sheer skirt, and sari fabric hip wrap in the style of Mata Hari.

Belt on top, bra underneath.

Belt On Top, Bra Underneath

For this style of ensemble, choose a loose, flowing beladi dress with a deep V-cut neckline. The bra is worn beneath the dress and can be viewed through the long center opening. The belt is worn over the top of the garment and holds the dress in place around the hips. A collar at the top connects to the gown with hooks and eyes, preventing the deep neck from sliding or slipping off the shoulders.

Worn With a Belt

In this style, a belt is worn over a dress that has an elaborately beaded neckline. The complexity of the surface design draws attention to the upper region. No performance bra is needed for this outfit. The dress can either have a built-in bra, or be worn with a lingerie bra that's sturdy enough for performance use. Some dresses are constructed with a built-in bra to support the dancer and prevent the dress from slipping, inadvertently showing the lingerie.

Embellished Dress

Another option is to create a dress that is a stand-alone performance garment. Although an infinite variety of cuts and shapes are available for a dancer, having applied surface embellishments that draw attention to the motion of the hips and bust is a must. This style of dress can be loose and flowing or fitted.

Dress worn with a belt.

Left: Embellished dress.
Above: Detail of belt fringe.

Basic Dress Shapes

In general, there are two basic shapes for dresses. The fitted dance gown skims and hugs the body, following the contours of the dancer's figure. From sexy slits to strategically placed cut-outs, the fitted evening gown style offers the designer a wide selection of features.

Alternatively, there are loose dress styles that are soft and fluid. Beladi dresses or tunics drape across the figure, skimming the body shapes and obscuring the contours of the figure. The belt is worn over these loose dress styles to draw attention to the hips.

Fitted Gowns

Although there are several specialty companies that sell patterns for beladi dresses and dance gowns, commercial pattern companies have a wide selection of dress styles that are well suited for adaptation into Middle Eastern dance wear. Look for styles that are fitted through the torso, but which also have full skirts or slits to allow for movement of the legs. If you like the look of stretch velvet or like the feel of clingy fabrics, make sure to buy a dress pattern that is designed with these fabrics in mind.

Fitted dresses require a closure, such as a zipper, snaps, or hooks. Look for design features that will enhance your figure. If you've got great legs, use styles with sexy slits. If you like your shoulders, show them off with asymmetrical necklines and "cold shoulder" features. Look for designs that have substantial straps that will stand up to the rigors of performance. Read the pattern envelope for suggested fabrics to get an idea of what types of cloth will work well. If you have your heart set on using a particular type of fabric, buying a pattern to suit the weave will save you a lot of headaches and adjustments.

Stretch Sheath

The stretch sheath can be used as either a foundation dress or alone when coated with decorative embellishments. There are many wonderful Spandex-blend fabrics for sheath dresses. These dresses cling and hug the body of the dancer, but stretch to allow the dancer a full range of movements. Some styles don't require a closure due to the stretchable nature of the Spandex-blend fabric, so the dress can simply slip over your head.

Fitted Sheath

These dresses are made from non-stretching cloth, so they require complex seaming to create their shape. Princess line seams are the most common style of seaming. Some dresses are cut with shaped sides and darts to fit the bust. Some dresses

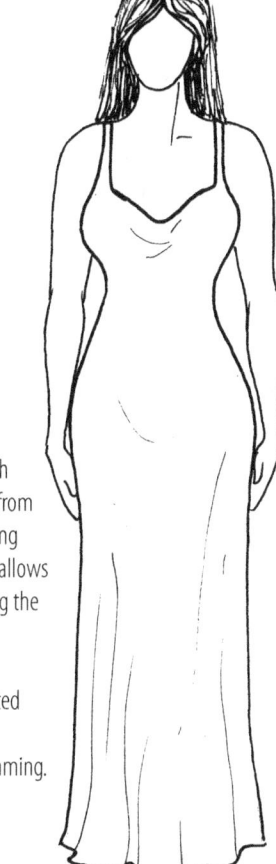

Right: The stretch sheath is made from a fabric containing Spandex which allows the gown to hug the body.

Far right: The fitted sheath shape is formed from seaming. This style uses princess lines.

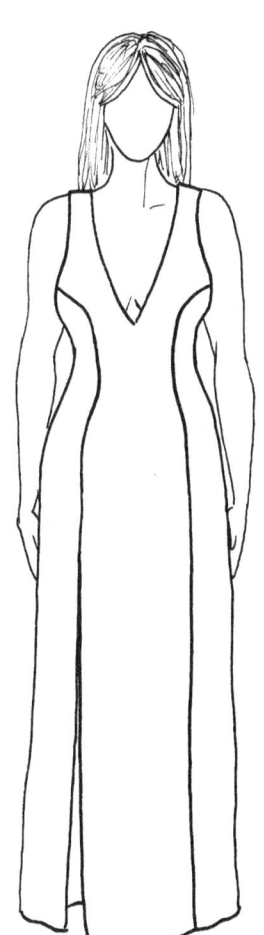

have shaped bodices with long sleek skirts that fall from an empire waistline. Many evening gown style dresses can be adapted. While you are pattern shopping consider styles with these features:

- Avoid fitted bodices or corset-like shaping.
- Look for body skimming styles that will show-off complex stomach work.
- Empire lines and princess style seaming will flatter most figure types.

Loose Dresses

Some dancers like to wear long, loose dresses that skim the body. They can be made of luxurious cloth, dripping with beads, or they can be constructed out of simple cotton fabrics. Loose dresses can be a versatile addition to the dancer's wardrobe. For those days when a dancer just wants to slip into something comfortable, or requires a bit more coverage, the loose dress is an instant costume. These dresses can also double as a between set cover in a pinch. In the loose-styled dress, the fabric needs to be soft with lots of drape. If the fabric is stiff, it will stand away from the body and add visual weight to the figure of the dancer.

Shimmy Dress

Shimmy dresses are just dripping with beaded fringe, paillettes, or chainette fringe that transforms into a shimmer of undulating light as soon as the dancer moves. If you plan on applying rows of paillettes, make sure they are attached using loose loops so that they have the freedom to flip and move in order to accent the dance. Inexpensive chainette fringe paired with washable fabric makes a dress that will take the dancer from practice to performance. When selecting a pattern, look for loose, semi-fitted shapes with simple body-skimming lines.

Tunic

A loose, flowing style, the dance tunic or beladi dress can be a wonderfully versatile addition to the dancer's wardrobe. If the tunic is loose enough, it can be worn with a bra and belt set, the bra being worn under the tunic while the belt is worn on top. Assuite is a popular fabric choice for a dance tunic. This precious fabric is a net impregnated with silver wrapped through the netting and pounded flat to become part of the cloth. A sheer tunic can be extremely effective to minimize body exposure when worn with a coordinating bra, belt, and pants. This look can vary from a high-glamour look to more folkloric styling depending on the choice of fabrics. Tunics don't require a pattern since they are based on a simple "T" shape and are made with rectangles cut to fit your hip and length measurements.

Above left: Shimmy dress.
Left: The loose-fitting tunic.

Dresses From Other Dance Styles

Dresses from other dance styles offer more options for the Middle Eastern dancer to explore. Several different dance forms have dress styles that can work for the dancer interested in exploring crossover or fusion looks. Some styles, such as square dancing, probably won't offer a dancer much inspiration. However, some dance forms share a movement vocabulary or common stylistic features to make them viable for performance wear. Here are two examples, but keep your eyes peeled when watching any style of dance.

Ballroom Dance

The dresses worn for Latin dance can have many of the features of an elegant beladi dress. Exotic cut-outs, intricate beading, and skirts slit to the thigh are just a few of the design elements that will easily translate into beautiful dance garments for our style of dance. Also check with ballroom costume dealers for accessory pieces such as shoes, gloves, headgear and jewelry. Many vendors supply rhinestones and other decorative surface embellishments that can be a boon for the Middle Eastern dance costumer.

Flamenco Dance

The Flamenco style features long, full skirts suspended from fitted torsos. This style can be transformed into a Mediterranean fusion-style costume. With the addition of a hip wrap, belt, and some decorative trim or beading on the bodice, the focus of the viewer can be redirected. Even unadorned, the Flamenco costume can work effectively to support a Gypsy, Zambra-Mora, or Flamenco-fusion dance styles.

Transforming a Store-Bought Dress

Middle Eastern dance costuming can be quite expensive. Many dancers have learned to combat expense with creativity. Recycling old formal wear is a rite of passage for most dance costumers. Searching for the perfect beaded, sequined, elegant, and slinky gown to adapt for dance purposes can be challenging. But nothing beats the thrill of the hunt, the satisfaction of recycling, and the glory of appearing in a totally unique and gorgeous gown.

For many dancers, an old evening gown, bridal gown, or prom dress can form the basis for a fitted sheath, an elegant dance dress, or simple yardage for use in covering a bra and belt set. If you are planning on turning your find into a dance dress, here are some features to look for before purchasing a garment.

Good Fit

If the dress is too tight, you might split it during some of the more extreme movements of your dance. Remember: it's easier to take in, even if you have to take it in a lot, than to let out. A garment being purchased merely for its value as yardage must be large enough to suit your intended purpose for the project you have in mind. Take a tape measure with you when shopping and measure the garment to get a good idea if it will work for you.

Excellent Condition

You are creating this dress for a performance, so make sure to inspect the garment for obvious wear. Subtle imperfections might become glaring under stage lighting. Check for stains, strains, and loose threads in beadwork or seaming. Some of this can be repaired during the reconditioning process, but knowing ahead of time can prevent an unfortunate mishap. Especially sneaky are water spots on shiny satiny fabrics, body odors in acetate and polyester that cannot be removed, and loose beadwork that might give on the first serious spin.

Know Your Skills

No bargain is truly a bargain if you don't use it. Many a dancer has spotted the "perfect" dress in a thrift store or resale shop, only to find that the loose beading, strained appliqués, and awkward fit of the dress taxed their skills and resources. Paying someone else to refurbish your garment is one possible way to deal with this sort of unfortunate event, however it will offset the savings of recycling. If your skills are weak, but you would like to pursue this avenue, consult the bibliography and look for general reference books on sewing. It is possible to teach yourself how to sew. If you prefer a class, check your local community college, adult education service, and even your local fabric store for basic construction classes to get you started.

Inset: A prom dress.
Left: The prom dress, transformed. The lace overskirt was used to cover the bra, belt, collar, crown, and a pair of gauntlets. The appliqué at the chest was stitched on the back and a similar piece was made from lace scraps. Both were embellished with additional braids to tie them together.

15 Accessories

A simple costume can be worn with a skirt, bra, and belt. This is a minimalist look and can appear unfinished. Most dancers tie their ensembles together using accessory pieces. Accessories can range from footwear to head covers, jewelry and cover garments, and anything in between. There are several approaches to using accessories that extend and enhance a core wardrobe.

One Focal Point

One single, exciting accessory piece can add drama and provide a striking focal point for the ensemble. This can be as simple as a pair of opera-length gloves, one glittering crown, or a stunning necklace. Many dancers have parlayed this concept of a single focal point accessory into a signature piece. If you find you always wear a certain style of headdress or can't be without your tummy chain or arm poufs, why not play this up in your overall wardrobe by having variations on the theme available to coordinate with a variety of bedlah sets.

Coordinated Set

A set of simple, coordinated accessories can support the ensemble without drawing attention away from the costume. Simple headbands, cuffs, and ankle bands can give the dancer a finished look. These sets are often made from metallic cloth in a coordinating tone. Some dancers have accessory sets in silver, gold, copper, or in one of their favorite base colors, such as black, red, white, or any other color that dominates their wardrobe.

Matched Ensemble

Many dancers like the very uniform look of matching their accessories to their bra and belt sets. These ensembles are made from the same materials and motifs and carry the colors and textures out to the head, arms, and legs. Making a matched ensemble will transform even simplest bedlah set into a show-stopping costume.

Jewelry

Another option is to utilize jewelry as the principle accessories. They don't all have to match and a wardrobe of pieces can be built up over time. Coordinating the metals, gems, and beads will create the look of a set. For instance, a rhinestone necklace can be paired with rhinestone cuffs, earrings, and anklets even if the patterns don't match and the pieces are of varying quality. If you have a signature motif, such as a butterfly, heart, or even a repeated geometric pattern, look for pieces with these designs.

Accessory Types

There are a host of accessories that can enhance the look of an ensemble. Many accessories can be purchased and used as-is. Be creative when appropriating garments and jewelry from standard ready-to-wear. When you are selecting accessories, think about both your dance style and the features you wish to draw attention to. Here are a series of questions to get you started:

- What features do I want to accentuate and highlight?
- Do I perform moves that can be accented by accessories?
- Are there features I want to minimize by drawing attention in the opposite direction?
- Are my favorite costumes supported visually by a matching set of accessories?
- Do I want a wardrobe of accessories that coordinate with many different costumes?
- What style of costumes do I favor?
- Should my accessories support the overall style?

As you answer questions like these you will find that your accessory selection process goes much easier. Let the answers to the questions above guide you. For instance, if you are proud of your arm movements and want to accentuate them, then you will definitely want to consider accent pieces to wear on your arms. If you want to minimize a pair of unattractive ankles, you might want to purchase plain shoes that disappear under your skirt or pants rather than using anklets that would pull the eye downward.

If you have selected a particular theme, such as a Pharonic style, the obvious choice will be accessories that utilize ancient Egyptian designs. In our Pharonic costume shown here, one of the most distinctive features is the elaborate beaded collar. This kind of accessory wouldn't support every costume. But in this instance it's the focal point accessory that helps build the style.

In the rest of this chapter, I have broken down the accessories not by style, but by the location where they are worn on the body. Remember, style in accessories is about the surface design, the individual shape, and the motifs that are used to embellish these elements.

Head Gear and Hair Wear

Some dancers have lovely hair that they dance with, using it as if it were a prop. If that's the case with you, no other adornment is needed or required. For most dancers, however, accessorizing begins at the top. Headgear and hair ornamentation will draw the viewer's attention to the dancer's face. Petite dancer should always consider wearing a colorful, eye catching ornament to bring the eye up and enhance the visual appearance of height. Here are a few popular items that can be used to decorate the hair and head.

Head Bands

Popular with almost all styles of dance costume, the headband can be elaborately beaded, embellished with jewelry, or be as simple as a length of stretch elastic with sequins. It is easy to coordinate your headband with your costume. Because headbands are made from a narrow strip of cloth, it's easy to save enough of even the most precious fabric to make one. Similar to the headband is the hair scrunchy, which can be effective when it is wrapped around the base of a ponytail.

Crowns

More formal than a headband, the crown can be elaborately beaded with sequins and rhinestones. The crown shape is formed from a stiff interlayer of buckram and interfacing that supports the surface decoration. This structure creates a stiff, well-defined shape on the upper edge of the crown. An elastic band extends down and around the base of the skull to keep the crown comfortably secure. An alternative to the crown is a jeweled tiara. These can easily be found at wedding supply stores.

Hats

Decorative pillbox hats echo the shape of the fez, or the headdress worn by Barbara Eden when she starred in I Dream of Jeannie. Many commercial pattern companies sell patterns for hats that include pillbox styles. Look through the accessories and crafts sections of the latest pattern books to see if there is a pattern that can be adapted to your purposes.

Scarves

Scarves or veils can be simply tied around the head or held in place by a headband. Wearing a veil on the head can give your ensemble a nomadic flavor.

When draped over a pillbox hat, a fantasy harem style can be achieved. Veils for the head are often much smaller than the veils you might dance with. Some dancers like to wear their performance veil on their head, removing the headband to allow them to perform with the item.

A triangular kerchief that knots at the base of the skull can effectively accentuate a Mediterranean fusion style costume.

Hair Ornaments

These are embellished barrettes, clips, or combs that are worn in the hair to accent the costume. These can be as simple as a rhinestone-embellished clip or as complex as two barrettes with swags of beads suspended between. The beauty of this type of accessory is that they are simple to make from smallish scraps of cloth. A hot glue gun makes custom barrettes a fast and easy project. Shop your favorite department stores, especially during the holiday season, for hair jewelry you can import into your dance wardrobe. Check your favorite craft stores for books and direction sheets for barrette designs. Even commercial pattern companies have patterns for barrette embellishments.

Turbans

While the turban is perfectly appropriate for the tribal, folkloric, or historic dancer, creating a turban out of luxurious fabrics can be a great accent for a bedlah ensemble. Just remember that slick or metallic fabrics make poor choices for turbans because they are slippery. Fabric with lots of texture that grabs onto itself, such as a silk dupioni, cotton with lurex stripes, velvet, or even a crepe will work better than a smooth satin, charmouse, or crepe de' chine.

Neck Wear

Generally there are two basic options for neckwear accessory pieces. One is simply a necklace, such as a choker, drop, collar, or torque. Select a metal that will match the tones used in your costume. If you have chosen a necklace with beads or gems, match the colors or materials with your costume to build an integrated look. If you enjoy making beaded jewelry, there are many books on the market that have directions for projects that work well as a dance costume embellishment.

Alternatively, if you are making a coordinated set of accessories, you may want to make a choker or collar to match your complete ensemble. A choker can be as simple as a piece of decorative ribbon or braid, with a hook and eye to serve as a closure. If you want something a little more substantial to serve as a base for beading, appliqué, or complex trim application then a collar built from a strip of stiff interfacing, covered in coordinating fabric, will make a good sturdy base for the applied surface design.

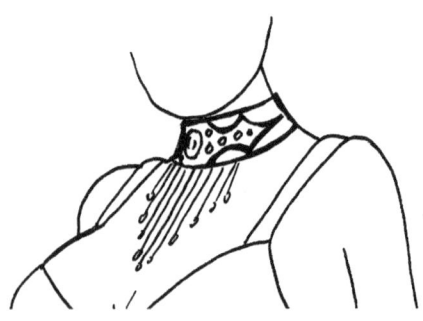

Arms and Wrists

Accenting the arms and wrists is a great way to pull the audience's eye out to the graceful movement of the arms. When planning arm decorations, consider what your goals are for this region. Some designs draw attention to the area, while others, through the art of redirection, pull the viewer's attention elsewhere.

Cuffs

These dramatic additions pull the viewer's eye to the movement of the hands. Cuffs are an excellent choice for the dancer who needs to conceal a watch tan line. When the arms are down at the side, cuffs might line up with the belt, adding visual width.

Gauntlets

The gauntlet reaches from wrist to elbow, covering the forearms. These can be made to match your costume or out of coordinating materials. Vendors carry beaded net, fringed, and jeweled styles, but you can make your own. For a fitted gauntlet made from stretch fabric, you can adapt an opera-length glove pattern with the palm and fingers removed.

Arm Poufs

Arm poufs are quite popular among dancers who want to add color and movement and yet need coverage for problem areas. Poufs can be made from nearly any fabric. Drapey materials will create graceful swoops while stiffer fabrics will create a bigger pouf, making areas look bigger than they really are. Poufs are based on a simple rectangle construction with a casing on each end. However, you can embellish them with slits, shaped cut outs, or attached ruffles.

Opera-Length Gloves

One of the hottest arm-accentuating styles is a pair of opera-length gloves. Gloves can be purchased at department stores with eveningwear departments, wedding shops, and specialty accessory shops. If you cannot find a pair to match or coordinate with your favorite costume, there are glove styles available through several major commercial pattern companies. Or try dying a pair of wedding gloves. Look for rayon, cotton, or silk gloves, which are easier to dye using home methods.

Sleeves

Some dancers like to keep the arms completely covered, from the bra strap down. Detachable sleeves can provide total coverage while integrating into multiple costume ensembles. One quick method for making a pair of sleeves is to purchase a commercial pattern for a raglan cut blouse. A loop at the top of the sleeve wraps around the bra strap attaching them to the costume. Use snaps to make the sleeves removable for easy laundering.

Bracelets and Arm Jewelry

Perhaps the easiest way to accentuate your arms is with jewelry. Bracelets and biceps cuffs are available from specialty vendors and even at your favorite department store. Having a selection of bracelets will extend your accessory wardrobe, as well as providing you with jewelry that can be worn beyond the realm of dance.

Stomach Covers

For dancers interested in concealing their stomachs there are several options that can integrate into a bedlah set without sacrificing the glamour. A beladi dress or evening gown style of ensemble offers good overall coverage of the tummy region. However, if you prefer the bedlah look, have existing costumes, or are coordinating with a troupe, here are some options for you.

Beaded Draping

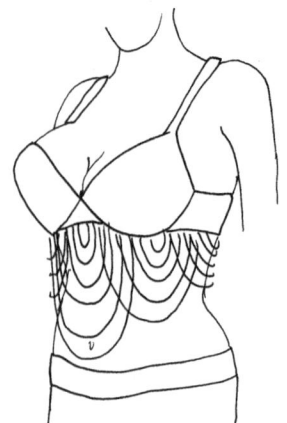

A significant beaded stomach drape can be integrated into the decoration of the bra. If you have an existing costume bra, you might be able to match your beads and add an elaborately beaded stomach drape to your costume. These can also be made to be removable so that you can wear them with a variety of different costumes. Mount the drape onto a tape and attach to the bra with hooks or snaps to make it usable with other costumes.

Body Stocking

Some dance vendors carry body stockings that can vary from body-length to torso covers that only span the area between the belt and bra. Body stockings are usually made from fabric with Spandex included. Stretch lace, power net, and stretch velvet are just a few of the textiles that make form-fitting tummy covers.

Fabric Drape

A loose fabric drape can match the skirts, accessories, or veils while providing coverage of the tummy area. This look is most effective when you use lightweight or semi-sheer fabrics that drape across the body and show the movements of the torso below. Avoid stiff fabrics like tissue lamé or crystal organza or heavy fabrics like loose velvet or brocade. These fabrics won't show subtle moves and will add visual bulk.

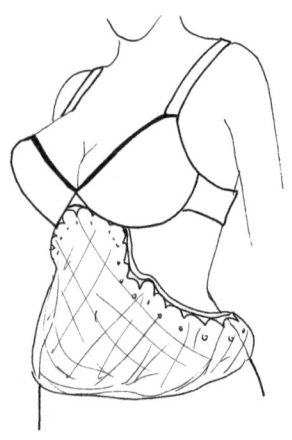

Top: Beaded stomach drape. Attach to a tape band and make removeable to use in multiple costumes.
Middle: Body stocking made from stretch lace.
Bottom: Fabric drape with tummy cover.

Shoes

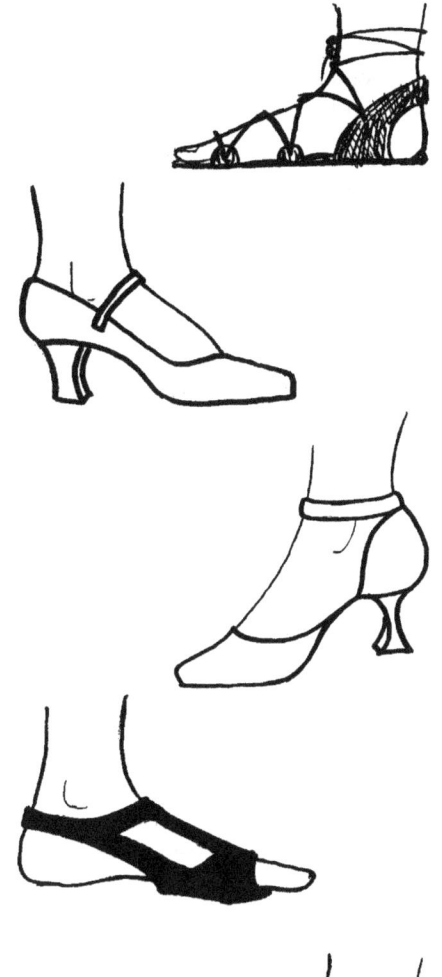

Dancing barefooted can be dangerous and should be avoided for the health and safety of your feet. Many dancers struggle to find suitable footwear that won't detract from the entire costume ensemble. Shoes designed specifically for dance purposes have soles that give the dancer control over the flex of the foot and the amount of slide during spins. These are some of the styles popular with Middle Eastern dancers.

Hermes Sandals

This style of shoe is worn by lyrical ballet dancers and is available at dance supply shops. These shoes have a smooth leather sole with tabs that curl around the foot and lace together across the toe and then around the ankle. There are similar styles sold by historical re-enactors with heavier rubber or leather soles.

Character Shoes

These are the standard of theatrical dancers and are worn for tap dancing, flamenco, and jazz dance. They come in a variety of heel heights in standard colors such as black, red, and tan. Because they are designed for dancers, they are very durable and can last for years.

Ballroom Dance Shoes

There are a wide variety of ballroom dance shoe styles available today. They range from the slinky, strappy Latin-style models to closed toe smooth shoes. Beautiful ballroom dance shoes come in luxurious fabrics with rhinestones, beads, shine, and glitz built onto a sole designed for dancing. These are an excellent choice for dancers who enjoy performing in heels.

Half Soles

Modern dancers like to rely on half soles to protect the balls of their feet during spins and yet preserve the flexibility on the arch and toes. This style of shoe does not provide the heel with support or protection, but in an environment where you trust the floor, this style is an option.

Mary Janes

This simple style of shoe has a closed toe with a strap across the instep. Some dancers like the Chinese style, made with velvet or cotton mounted on a plastic stole. Standard shoe stores carry modified Mary Janes. During the holiday season you might find pairs in luxurious, decorative fabrications.

Ghillies

These shoes are Celtic in origin and are worn in Irish and Scottish step dancing. However, this style is very comfortable, supportive, and will allow you to spin easily. They also coordinate beautifully with many styles of Middle Eastern dance wear.

Ballet Slippers

Some dancers like to wear ballet slippers. They are available in a wide range of colors from specialty vendors. Some shoes are dyeable and can be transformed in color to match any costume style. They are also available in standard metallic tones.

Jazz Shoes

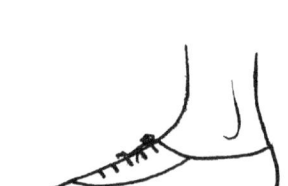

These oxford style shoes can be a comfortable style to integrate with Mediterranean fusion style costumes. They have a sturdy sole and a slight heel that offers the dancer a little bit of lift without adding a lot of height.

There are many other options that I have not illustrated here. They include ethnic slippers, fancy embellished pumps, and sandals. Can't match your costume? Have no fear! Wedding shoes come in a wide variety of shapes and styles and can be dyed to match. Sequins, beads, and rhinestones can be added using adhesive products to create a completely coordinated look.

Cover-ups

Many dancers have to arrive at their performance venue wearing their costume. Others have a long walk from the changing room, through the audience, to the performance space. To preserve the surprise of a dramatic entrance, you need a loose cover-up to prevent the audience from sneaking a peek. There are many options in styles and shapes. Following is a list of the most common.

Aba

This Middle Eastern garment is composed of a long rectangle of cloth that folds to create the shoulder and arm line and opens in the front. This garment style can be made out of all sorts of fabrics, from lightweight georgette to heavy velvet. Closures can be as simple as a hook and eye, ties, buttons, or frogs. Use your height, and the span of your arms from wrist to wrist to establish your sizes. If you cannot find fabric this wide, simply place a seam up the center back.

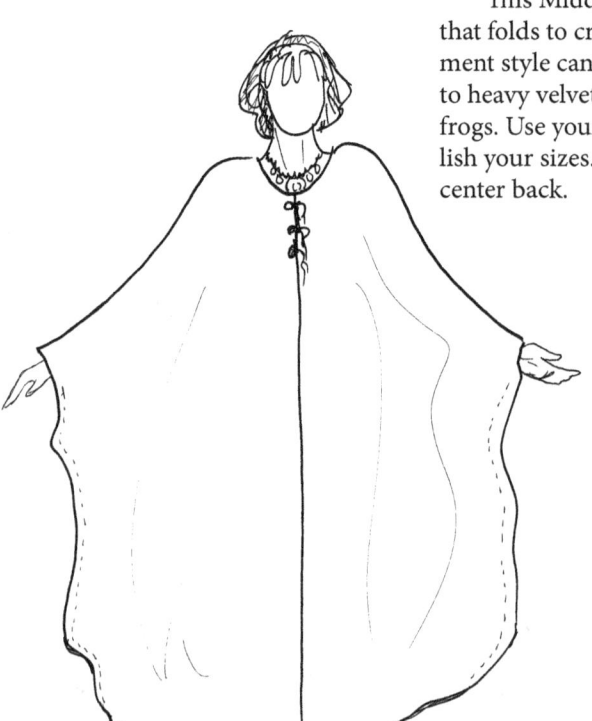

Aba

Accessories

Khaftan

Khaftan

A shaped khaftan that either opens down the front, or fits over the head, can be a nice way of integrating a more ethnic look into a cover-up. These types of garments can be made from any fabric, although traditional garments are made from cotton embellished with embroidery, shells, mirrors, coins, beads, or buttons. These garments are generally made from the measurements of the body rather than from patterns, but there are companies that make patterns for similar styled garments. Check out the options available from Folkwear patterns and other commercial companies that might have modern adaptations of these traditional styles.

Capes

One garment that can be a versatile addition to the dancer's wardrobe is the cape. A cape can be made as a durable garment with a lining and slits for the arms to pass through, or it can be just a simple single layer. Many different commercial companies have cape patterns that don't even need alteration to develop into a suitable cover-up. The beauty of the cape is that it can be beaded or embellished at the shoulder line to add a little glamour. Conversely, a cape can be made from sturdy durable cloth and used for other purposes than merely a dance cover-up.

Veils

One item that bridges the space between prop and costume is the veil. An elegant way to conceal the costume is to wrap one or more veils around the body. Many dancers perform with either single or double veils as a portion of a long performance. There are many different veils available commercially through specialty dance vendors. However, a veil can be as simple as a length of cloth with a hem on each end. There is no set formula for making a veil. Generally, you want your veil to be longer than your arms at full extension, gracefully draping beyond the fingertips. If your veil is shorter, it will limit your movements. Creating your veil out of soft, fluid fabrics will make a veil that flows and drapes elegantly. Stiffer, more substantial fabrics lend themselves to shaped veils and large swooping motions. No matter if you are making a simple rectangular veil, a semi circular veil, or a shaped veil, make sure that edges are hemmed so that if your veil winds up floating into the audience they will see a well-finished product.

Cape

Veil wrap

16 Care and Storage

Once you have completed your costume, you are ready to perform. During performances, costume pieces get sweaty and dirty. Middle Eastern dance costumes are complex garments that can be extremely difficult to launder. Many beads and most sequins will not handle more than a buffing with damp cloth. Lamé and velvet, while dry cleanable, are often loaded up with bangles and trim that are difficult to wash. Care for your costume in the manner appropriate for its construction materials in order to extend its working life as long as possible.

After each performance, treat your costume to some tender loving care. Develop a routine to preserve each costume piece and extend its life. Here is a quick list to get you started. Every dancer has their unique method for costume care and storage. Ask your favorite dancer how she keeps her costumes in mint condition.

When Your Costume Is New

Make all linings removable. Put the lining on the garment last and take it out when it looks worn, smelly, stained, or damaged. The lining of the bra and belt are pressed tightly to your flesh and absorb perspiration readily. Change the linings frequently to extend the life of your garment. If you perspire freely, you may want to consider including a layer of plastic, rubber, or latex between your costume and the inner lining.

Make a test sample composed of all materials in your costume. Hand wash this sample to see how the costume will fare through the washing process. Pay attention to how the materials respond to cleansing. Be especially aware that some sequins, coins, and beads can lose their color when in contact with perspiration or even water. So make sure to test, test, test. If you are placing sequins or coins in locations where they will touch the body, seal them with clear lacquer or acrylic spray paint to help protect them from harmful contact.

If you have costume pieces you want to wash, such as head scarves, body stockings, or a chemise, make sure to test wash all materials and decorations before you make them. If you have purchased these items, begin by test washing a portion by hand. Be careful in your testing. Once you have determined the best washing method, wash them as soon as you can after a performance.

To extend the life of costumes with Egyptian fringe, prepare the fringe before wearing. At the bottom of each strand, apply a layer of clear nail polish, super glue, or other clear adhesive. This will strengthen the knot. If possible, use this technique at the top as well. If you have hand-beaded your own fringe, this is a good precaution that can preserve your work.

When You Are Dancing

Keep away from flames. Candles on tables, cigarettes in ashtrays, and any flaming dishes should be avoided. Not only could your costume burn or melt, so could you. Nylon and polyester will melt and stick to your skin when in close proximity to extreme heat or flame. Silk, cotton, and wool will smolder or burn. Think safety when you perform. Remove risks before they remove you.

Know your costume well. Nothing is sadder than to see a dancer damage her own costume during a performance. Make sure that your costume fits well. Dance in it during practice to find out where its limitations are. Note any moves that cannot be completed safely in the costume and remove them from your routine. For example, don't do the splits in a straight, fitted skirt.

A beautiful costume that took ages to make, or cost a lot of cash, could be easily ruined when doing floor work on an unclean surface. Even a floor that appears immaculately clean will have a layer of dirt across it. If you have a chance, sweep before a performance so you can minimize the amount of grime your beads and sequins will pick up. Carpets are particularly challenging because they suck up dirt and can catch on beads. You wouldn't roll around in a beaded Dior or a sequined Versace. Protect your investment by making choices about your dance performance.

After a Performance

Lay your costume up to dry. Make sure that all pieces are adequately supported to avoid unnecessary strain. Mesh drying racks work well and allow for good airflow. Never put a moist or damp costume away. Mildew can eat away slowly at any natural fibers and it thrives in dark, damp fabric.

Inspect the surface of your garment. By spotting any food remains, tears, loose beads or coins, raveling fringe, and other loose trim, you can make the repairs or cleaning at once. If you let a stain sit, it stays. If you see a coin getting loose, you can repair it before it disappears in a whirl. Beads fall off costumes all of the time. By taking precautions ahead of time you can prevent more of your decorations from flying away.

Many dancers use a fragrant deodorant on their skin that in turn rubs off onto their costumes. Other dancers spritz their costumes with perfume to mask unwanted body odors and keep them as fresh smelling as they are fresh looking. A light dusting of cornstarch over the lining will also do the trick. Burning candles or incense below your costume as it is airing will also freshen the garment. Another method is to use a solution of half water and half vodka in a spray bottle. Spray the inside of your costume with this solution before you dance. This is an old theatre trick that changes and cuts through the odor of perspiration. There are new products in the cleaning aisle at the supermarket that are designed to cut through odors with a spray application.

Don't wear the same costume over and over again. By having at least two costumes you can rotate them, extending the life of each individual garment. This will also give you down time for each costume so you can make repairs, change linings, and revamp the decorations.

Storage

Store costumes with dangling beads and bias-cut skirts by laying them flat. This may be difficult, as storage space seems to be a problem for everyone. However, gravity will pull on skirt hems and hanging beads even after the closet door is shut. Circular skirts can develop uneven hems when left to hang for long periods of time. Strands of beads can stretch, too, letting the threads show, or worse yet, break.

To extend the life of your garments, store them in boxes or bags that allow the circulation of air. This will help keep the costume from getting musty and hold down levels of mold and mildew. Also, avoid placing your costume in acidic boxes or touching wooden items. These can cause discoloration during long-term storage.

Place a desiccant such as silica gel in your storage boxes to minimize mildew and mold growth. Include a fabric bag of baking soda or cornstarch to absorb odors and moisture from the air. Some sports stores also sell products that are designed to deodorize shoes and other athletic equipment. Try to maintain good air circulation to prevent the growth of mildew.

Periodically clean and inspect the bag that you carry your costumes in to and from performances. Check for sharp edges, holes that can allow dirt to get on your costumes, or tears in linings that can swallow small accessories and jewelry. Keep your bag clean. Keep the products you carry that could possibly harm your costumes, such as perfume, deodorant, or cosmetics, in a separate sealed bag.

Many of these tips you have heard before. Most are common sense. If you feel that you are pressed for time and cannot follow through on the care of your garment, consider the amount of money and time you have invested in it. Consider the way that a well-fitted, beautiful costume can enhance your performances. Belly dancing requires an exotic as well as professional image. Don't let your costume down and it won't let you down.

Beadwork Template

Bibliography

For a more complete and updated bibliography visit my website at www.davina.us.

Dance and Performance – History and Instruction

Al-Rawi, Rosina-Fawzia, B. and Monique Arav. *Grandmother's Secrets: The Ancient Rituals and Healing Power of Belly Dance.* Interlink Publishing: Northhampton, MA 1999.

Andes, Karen. *A Woman's Book of Power: Using Dance to Cultivate Energy.* Perigee: Berkeley 1998.

Bernstein, Matthew. *Visions of the East: Orientalism in Film.* Rutgers University Press: New Brunswick, NJ 1997.

Buonaventura, Wendy. *Serpent Of The Nile: Women and Dance in the Arab World.* Interlink Books: New York 1989.

Buonaventura, Wendy. *The Serpent and the Sphinx.* Lodon: Virago 1983.

Carlton, Donna. *Looking for Little Egypt.* IDD Books: Bloomington, IN 1994.

Dahlena and Dona Z. Meilach. *The Art of Belly Dancing.* Bantam Books: Toronto 1975.

Djoumahna, Kajira. *The Tribal Bible.* Kajira Djoumahna's Black Sheep Books, Bodywork and Bazaar: Santa Rosa, CA 1999.

Gioseffi, Daniela. *Earth Dancing, Mother Nature's Oldest Rite.* Stackpole Book: Harrison, PA 1980.

Hobin, Tina and Kristyna K'ashvili. *Belly Dancing: For Health and Relaxation.* Focus Publishing: NY 1982.

Richards, Tazz, ed. *The Belly Dance Book: Rediscovering the Oldest Dance.* Backbeat Press: Concord, CA 2000.

Lexova, Irena. *Ancient Egyptian Dances.* Dover Publications: New York 2000.

Long, Rob. *Belly Laughs: Adventures with Celebrities and Other Unusual Characters.* Talion Pub.: Renton, WA 1999.

Mishkin, Julie Russo. *The Compleat Belly Dancer.* Garden City: New York 1973.

Nieuwkerk, Karin van. *A Trade Like Any Other: Female Singers and Dancers in Egypt.* University of Texas Press: Austin, TX 1995.

Serena and Alan Wilson. *The Serena Technique of Belly Dancing.* Pocket Books: New York 1974.

Stewart, Iris. *Sacred Women, Sacred Dance: Awakening Spirituality Through Movement and Ritual.* Inner Traditions Intl. Ltd. 2000.

Costume and Textile History

At the Edge of Asia: Five Centuries of Turkish Textiles. Santa Barbara Museum of Art: Santa Barbara, CA 1983.

Askari, Nasreen. *Uncut Cloth.* Merrell Holberton Publishers: London 1999.

Askari, Nasreen and Rosemary Crill. *Colors of the Indus.* The Victoria and Albert Museum in conjunction with Merrell Holberton Publishers: London 1997.

Baker, Patricia. *Islamic Textiles.* British Museum Press: London 1995.

Besancenot, Jean. *Costumes of Morocco.* Kegan Paul International: London 1990.

Bijutsu, Indo Senshoku, and Kokyo Hatanaka. *Textiles Arts of India: Kokyo Hatanaka Collection.* Chronicle Books: San Francisco 1996.

Biswas, A. *Indian Costumes.* Publications Division, Ministry of Information and Broadcasting, Govt. of India: New Delhi 1985.

Boucher, François. *20,000 Years of Fashion.* Abrams: New York 1987.

Boulanger, Chantal. *Saris: An Illustrated Guide to the Indian Art of Draping.* Shakti Press International: 1997.

Burnham, Dorothy K. *Cut My Cote.* Royal Ontario Museum: Ontario 1973.

Brij Bhushan, Jamila. *Indian Embroidery.* Publications Ministry, Ministry of Information and Broadcasting, Govt. of India: New Delhi 1990.

Clothing and Difference: Embodied Identities in Colonial and Post-Colonial Africa. Hildi Hendrickson, ed. Duke University Press: Durham 1996.

Crill, Rosemary. *Indian Ikat Textiles.* Weatherhill: London 1998.

Crill, Rosemary. *Indian Embroidery.* V&A Publications: London 1999.

Das, Sukla. *Fabric Art: Heritage of India.* South Asia Books 1992.

Elson, Vickie C. *Dowries form Kutch.* Museum of Cultural History, University of California: Los Angeles 1979.

From the Far West: Carpets and Textiles of Morocco. Textile Museum: Washington 1980.

Guy, John. *Woven Cargoes: Indian Textiles in the East.* Thames and Hudson 1998.

Gillow, John and Nicholas Barnard. *Traditional Indian Textiles.* Thames and Hudson 1993.

Harvey, Janet. *Traditional Textiles of Central Asia.* Thames and Hudson:London 1996.

Kumar, Ritu. *Costumes and Textiles of Royal India.* Manson & Woods: 1999.

Laver, James. *Costume & Fashion: A Concise History.* Thames and Hudson: London 1985.

Leese, Elizabeth. *Costume Design in the Movies.* Dover: New York 1991.

Lynton, Linda. *The Sari, Styles, Patterns, History, Technique.* Harry N. Abrams: New York 1995.

Mackie, Louise W. *The Splendor of Turkish Weaving: An Exhibition of Silks and Carpets of the 13th–18th Centuries.* The Textile Museum: Washington, D. C. 1973.

Maeder, Edward. *Hollywood and History.* Thames and Hudson/Los Angeles County Museum of Art: Los Angeles 1987.

Markaz al-Funun wa-al-Taqalid al-Sha'biyah. *Les Costumes Traditionnels Feminins de Tunisie.* Maison Tunisienne de L'edition: Tunis 1988.

Martin, Richard and Harold Koda. *Orientalism: Visions of the East in Western Dress.* Metropolitan Museum of Art: New York 1994.

Mayer, L. A. Mamluk *Costume: a Survey.* A. Kundig: Geneve 1952.

Museum of International Folk Art. A Portfolio of Folk Costume, Volumes One and Two. Museum of New Mexico Press: New Mexico 1971.

Naik, Shailaja D. Traditional *Embroideries of India.* South Asia Books: Columbia, MO 1996.

Rajab, Jehan S. *Palestinian Costume.* Kegan Paul International: London 1989.

Rivers, Victoria Z. *The Shining Cloth.* Thames and Hudson: London 1999.

Reswick, Irmtraud. *Tradtional Textiles of Tunisia and Related North African Weavings.* Craft & Folk Art Museum: Los Angeles 1985.

Rogers, J. M. *The Topkapi Saray Museum, Costumes, Embroideries, and Other Textiles.* Thames and Hudson: London 1986.

Ross, Heather Colyer. *The Art of Arabian Costume: A Saudi Arabian Profile.* Arabesque Commercial: Montreux, Switzerland 1981.

Scarce, Jennifer. *Women's Costume of the Near and Middle East.* Unwin Hyman: London 1987.

Spring, Christopher. *North African Textiles.* British Museum Press: London 1995.

Stillman, Yedida Kalfon. *Palestinian Costume and Jewelry.* University of New Mexico Press: Albuquerque, NM 1979.

Tilke, Max. *Folk Costumes from East Europe, Africa, and Asia.* A. Zwemmer: London 1978.

Weir, Shelagh. *Palestinian Costume.* British Museum Publications LTD: London 1989.

Woven from the Soul, Spun from the Heart: Textile Arts of Safavid and Qajar Iran, 16th-19th Centuries. The Textile Museum: Washington, D.C. 1987.

Yarwood, Dooreen. *The Encyclopedia of World Costume.* Bonanza Books: New York 1986.

Jewelry

Andrews, Carol. *Amulets of Ancient Egypt.* University of Texas Press: Austin 1994.

Andrews, Carol. *Ancient Egyptian Jewelry.* Harry N. Abrams: New York 1990.

Beck, Horace. *Classification and Nomenclature of Beads and Pendants.* George Shumway Publisher: York, PA 1981.

Borel, France and John Bigelow Taylor. *The Splendor of Ethnic Jewelry.* Harry N. Abrams: New York 1994.

Butor, Michel. *Ethnic Jewelry: Africa, Asia and the Pacific.* Rizzoli: New York 1994.

Boyer, Martha Haensen and Ida Nicolaisen. *Mongol Jewelry.* Thames and Hudson: London 1995.

D'Orey, Leonor. *Five Centuries of Jewellery.* Scala Books: Lisbon 1996.

Evens, Joan. *A History of Jewellery, 1100-1870.* Dover: New York 1970.

Fisher, Angela. *Africa Adorned.* Harry N. Abrams: New York 1984.

Hasson, Rachel. *Early Islamic Jewellery.* Institute for Islamic Art: Jerusalem 1987.

Hasson, Rachel. *Later Islamic Jewellery.* Institute for Islamic Art: Jerusalem 1987.

Higgens, Reynold. *Greek and Roman Jewellery.* Methuen and Co. LTD.: London 1980.

Islamic Jewelry in the Metropolitan Museum of Art. Metropolitan Museum of Art: New York 1983.

Mack, John. *Ethnic Jewelry.* Harry N. Abrams: New York 1988.

Meilach, Dona Z. *Ethnic Jewelry: Design & Inspiration for Collectors and Craftsmen.* Crown Publishers: New York 1981.

Ross, Calyer Heather. *The Art of Bedouin Jewellery, A Saudi Arabian Profile.* Arabesque: Frisbourg, Switzerland 1981.

Tait, Hugh. *Jewelry, 7,000 Years.* Abradale Press: New York 1991.

Untracht, Oppi. *Traditional Jewelry of India.* Harry N. Abrams: New York 1997

Beads, Beadwork, and Applied Surface Design

Benson, Ann. *Beadwork Basics.* Sterling Publishing Co: New York 1995.

Campbell-Harding, Valeria and Pamela Watts. *Bead Embroidery.* Lacis Publications: Berkeley, CA 1993.

Coles, Janet. *The Book of Beads.* Simon and Schuster: New York 1990.

Conlon, Jane. *Fine Embellishment Techniques.* The Taunton Press: Newtown, CT 1999.

Crutchley, Anna and Tim Imrie. *The Tassels Book.* Lorenz books: New York 1996.

Dryden, Deborah. *Fabric Painting and Dyeing for the Theatre.* Heinemann: Portsmouth, NH 1993.

Dubin, Lois Sherr. *The History of Beads: From 30,000 B.C. to the Present.* H. N. Abrams: New York 1987.

Dunnewold, Jane. *Complex Cloth: A Comprehensive Guide to Surface Design.* Martingale & Co.Inc.: Woodinville, WA 1996.

Durant, Judith & Jean Campbell. *The Beader's Companion.* Interweave Press: Loveland, CO 1998.

Eaton, Jan. *The Complete Stitch Encyclopedia.* Quarto Publishing: London 1995.

Eichorn, Rosemary. *The Art of Fabric Collage.* Taunton Press: Newtown CT 2000.

El-Khalidi, Laila. *The Art of Palestinian Embroidery.* Al Saqi 1999.

Grewal, Neelam. *The Needle Lore: Traditional Embroideries of Kashmir, Himachal Prdesh, Punjab, Haryana, Rajasthan.* Ajanta Publications: Delhi 1988.

Hill, Wendy. *On the Surface: Thread Embellishments and Fabric Manipulation.* C&T Publishing: Lafayette, CA 1997.

Johnstone, Pauline. *Greek Island Embroidery.* H.M.S.O.: London 1972.

Johnstone, Pauline. *Turkish Embroidery.* Victoria & Albert Museum: London 1985.

Kling, Candice. *The Artful Ribbon.* C&T Publishing: Lafayette CA 1997.

McGehee, Linda. F. *Creating Textures with Textiles.* Krause Publications: Iola, WI 1998.

Murrah, Judy. *Jazz It Up: 101 Stitching & Embellishing Techniques.* Martingale & Co. Inc. 1999.

Laurty, Jean Ray. *Imagery on Fabric.* C&T Publishing: Lafayette CA 1997.

Morrell, Anne. *Techniques of Indian Embroidery.* B.T. Batsford: London 1994.

Noble, Elin. ***Dyes & Paints: A Hands-On Guide to Coloring Fabric.*** Martingale & Co. Inc: Woodinville, WA 1998.

Taylor, Carol. ***Creative Bead Jewelry.*** Sterling Publishing, Inc.: New York 1995.

Valley, Stephanie. ***Embellishments A to Z: An Embellishment Idea Book.*** Taunton Press: Newtown, CT 1999.

Wilson, Ruth. ***Beautiful Beading.*** Sally Milner Publishing: Bowral, Australia 1999.

Withers, Sara. ***Exotic Beads.*** Krause Publications: Iola, WI 1996.

Weir, Shelagh. ***Palestinian Embroidery: A Village Arab Craft.*** British Museum: London 1970.

Wells, Kate. ***Fabric Dyeing and Printing.*** Interweave Press: Loveland, CO 1997.

Wolff, Colette. ***The Art of Manipulating Fabric.*** Krause Publications: Iola, WI 1996.

Pattern Making, Sewing, and Costume Design

Armstrong, Helen Joseph. ***Draping for Apparel Design.*** Fairchild Publications: New York 2000.

Armstrong, Helen Joseph. ***Patternmaking for Fashion Design.*** Harper & Row: New York 1987.

Amaden-Crawford, Connie. ***The Art of Fashion Draping.*** Fairchild Publishers: New York 1995.

Anderson, Barbara and Cletus. ***Costume Design.*** Holt, Rinehart and Winston: New York 1984.

Bensussen, Rusty. ***Making Patterns from Finished Clothes.*** Sterling Publications: New York 1985.

Bensussen, Rusty. ***Shortcuts to A Perfect Sewing Pattern.*** Sterling Publications: New York 1989.

Betzina, Sandra. ***Fabric Savvy.*** The Taunton Press: Newtown, CT 1999.

Butterick Pattern's Editor. ***The Vogue/Butterick Step-by-Step Guide to Sewing Techniques.*** Butterick Company: New York 1998.

Covey, Liz and Rosemary Ingham. ***The Costume Designer's Handbook.*** Heinemann Educational Books: Portsmouth, NH 1992.

Doyle, Tracy. ***Patterns from Finished Clothes: Re-creating the Clothes You Love.*** Sterling Publications: New York 1996.

Holkeboer, Katherine Strand. ***Costume Construction.*** Prentice Hall: Englewood Cliffs NJ 1989.

Jaffe, Hilde. ***Draping for Fashion Design.*** Prentice Hall: New York 1993.

Kopp, Ernestine, et all. ***Designing Apparel Through the Flat Pattern.*** Fairchilds Publishers: New York 1991.

Larkey, Jan. *Flatter Your Figure.* Simon & Shuster: New York 1991.

Readers Digest. *Complete Guide to Sewing.* The Reader's Digest Association, Inc.: Pleasantville, NY 1995.

Schaeffer, Claire. *Fabric Sewing Guide.* Krasue Publications, Iola WI 1994.

Singer. *Creative Sewing Ideas.* Singer: Minnetonka, MN 1990.

Singer. *Sewing Essentials.* Singer: Minnetonka, MN 1989.

Singer. *Sewing for Special Occasions.* Singer: Minnetonka, MN 1994.

Singer. *Sewing Specialty Fabrics.* Cy Decosse Incorporated: Minnetonka, MN 1986.

Tate, sharon Lee. *Inside Fashion Design.* Harper & Row Pub.: New York 1989.

Taylor, Enid. *Tassel Making for Beginners.* Sterling Publications: New York 1998.

Vogue. *Vogue Sewing.* Butterick Publishing Co: New York 2000.

Welsh, Nancy. *The Creative Art of Tassels.* Sterling Publications: New York 1999.

Wingate, Isabel B. and June F. Mohler. *Textile Fabrics and Their Selection.* Prentice Hall: New York 1984.

Clip Art, Design References, and Art Historical Sources

Abas, S. J. *Symmetries of Islamic Geometrical Patterns.* World Scientific: New Jersey 1995.

Akar, Axade. *Authentic Turkish Designs.* Dover Publications: New York 1992.

Akar Azade. *Treasury of Turkish Designs.* Dover Publications, Inc.: New York 1988.

Allane, Lee. *Oriental Rugs: A Buyers Guide.* Thames and Hudson: London 1988.

Alloula, Malek. *The Colonial Harem.* University of Minnesota Press: Minneapolis 1986.

Ammoun, Denise. *Crafts of Egypt.* American University of Cairo Press: Cairo 1991.

Barnard, Nicholas. *Arts and Crafts of India.* Conran Octopus: London 1993.

Blackman, Winifred. *The Fellahin of Upper Egypt.* G. G. Harrap & Co. Ltd.: London 1927.

Bloom, Jonathan and Sheila S. Blair. *Islamic Arts.* Phaidon Press: New York 1997.

Brend, Barbara. *Islamic Art.* Harvard University Press: Cambridge, Mass. 1991.

Buourgoin, J. *Islamic Patterns.* Dover Publications, Inc.: New York 1978.

Clevenot, Dominique. *Splendors of Islam.* Vendome Press: Paris

Davies, Peter. *The Tribal Eye: Antique Kilims of Anatolia.* Rizzoli: New York 1993.

Eastern Encounters: Orientalist Painters of the Nineteenth Century. Fine Art Society, Ltd.: London 1978.

Farooqi, Anis. *Art of India and Persia.* D. K. Publishers' Distributors: New Delhi 1979.

Field, Robert. *Geometric Patterns from Islamic Art & Architecture.* Tarquini Publications. 1999.

Gantzhorn, Volkmar. *Oriental Carpets.* Taschen: New York 1998.

Grafton, Carol Belanger. *Egyptian Designs.* Dover Publications, Inc.: New York 1993.

Hamann, Bradford R. *The Greek Design Book.* Stemmer House Publishers: Owings Mills, MA 1980.

Hillenbrand, Robert. *Islamic Art and Architecture.* Thames and Hudson: London 1998.

Hofmann, Richard. *Decorative Flower and Leaf Designs.* Dover: NY 1991.

Irwin, Robert. *Islamic Art in Context: Art, Architecture and the Literary World.* Harry N. Abrams: New York 1997.

Islam in the Balkans: *Persian Art and Culture of the 18th and 19th Centuries.* Royal Scottish Museum: Edinburgh 1979.

Jereb, James F. *Arts and Crafts of Morocco.* Chronicle Books: San Francisco 1995.

Khalter, Johannes. *The Arts and Crafts of Syria.* Thames and Hudson: London 1992.

Khalter, Johannes. *The Arts and Crafts of Turkestan.* Thames and Hudson: New York 1983.

Khalter, Johannes. *Heirs to the Silk Road: Uzbekistan.* Thames and Hudson: New York 1997.

Leland, Nita. *Exploring Color.* North Light Books: Cincinnati, OH 1998.

Lewis, Barnard. *The World of Islam: Faith, People, Culture.* W. W. Norton & Co.: New York 1992.

Lewis, Reina. *Gendering Orientalism: Race, Femininity and Representation.* Routledge: New York 1996.

MacKenzie, John M. *Orientalism: History, Theory and the Arts.* Manchester University Press: Manchester 1995.

Peltre, Christine. *Orientalism in Art.* Abbeville Press, Inc.: New York 1998.

Bibliography

Pope, Arthur Upham. *A Survey of Persian Art from Prehistoric Times to the Present.* Oxford University Press: London 1964-65.

Revault, Jactues. *Designs & Patterns from North African Carpets & Textiles.* Dover Publications Inc.: 1973.

Rice, David T. *Constantinople from Byzantium to Istanbul.* Stein and Day: New York 1965.

Rice, David T. *Islamic Art.* Praeger: New York 1965.

Rogers, J. M. *Mughal Miniatures.* Thames and Hudson: London 1993.

Simakoff, N. *Islamic Designs in Color.* Dover Publications: New York 1993.

Thompson, James. *The East, Imagined, Experienced, Remembered: Orientalist Nineteenth Century Painting.* National Gallery of Ireland: Dublin 1988.

Thornton, Lynne. *Women as Portrayed in Orientalist Painting.* ACR Edition: Paris 1985.

Titley, Norah M. *Persian Painting: Fourteenth Century.* Marg/Arnold-Heinemann: New Delhi 1977.

Topham, John. *Traditional Crafts of Saudi Arabia.* Stacey International: London 1981.

Valcarenghi, Dario. *Kilim: History and Symbols.* Electa 1994.

Vogel, Lucien. *Moroccan Silk Designs in Full Color.* Dover Publications Inc: New York 1996.

Welch, Stuart Cary. *Persian Painting.* George Braziller: New York 1996.

Wilson, Eva. *Ancient Egyptian Designs for Artists and Craftspeople.* Dover Publications, Inc.: New York 1987.

Wilson, Eva. *Islamic Designs for Artists and Craftspeople.* Dover Publications, Inc.: New York 1988.

Hand of Fatima

www.ingramcontent.com/pod-product-compliance
Lightning Source LLC
Chambersburg PA
CBHW081840170426
43199CB00017B/2793